GARDEN COLOR SERIES

ROCK GARDENS & ALPINE PLANTS

ROCK GARDENS & ALPINE PLANTS

David Joyce

ARCO PUBLISHING, INC.
New York

Endpapers *Raised alpine beds are an attractive way of growing a selection of rock plants in a limited space.*

Title page *An abundance of different flowering plants in the rock garden in summer, can be the highlight of your garden.*

Right *A well-planned rock garden with a balanced selection of flowering and evergreen plants can be a joy all year round.*

American Editor: Edwin F. Steffek

Published by Arco Publishing, Inc.
215 Park Avenue South, New York, N.Y. 10003

Copyright © 1985 by Marshall Cavendish Limited

Library of Congress Cataloging in Publication Data
Joyce, David.
    Rock gardens and alpine plants.

1. Rock gardens.   2. Alpine garden plants.   I. Title.
SB459.J69 1985   635.9'672   84–21636

ISBN 0–668–06409–9 (cloth)
ISBN 0–668–06413–7 (paper)

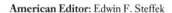

Printed in Hong Kong

CONTENTS

INTRODUCTION
Page 4

INTRODUCTION

Creating an attractive rock garden with many different varieties of plants, although initially hard work, can be a very satisfying project for everyone to enjoy.

There can be few with a genuine love of plants who have not been tempted to create in their own garden a home for alpines and rock plants. Despite the harshness of mountainous and rocky landscapes, these are the natural environments of some of the loveliest wild plants. The inhospitable conditions they have to survive include thin soils, sharp drainage, searing winds, frequent low temperatures and, in the alpine zone, snow cover during part of the year. At first, therefore, it is surprising to find that some of these natural landscapes convey the impression of a managed garden.

The plants have had to make many adaptations to cope with these hostile conditions but the most characteristic is a compact or ground-hugging habit of growth. It is this characteristic that gives alpine and rock plants their managed appearance in the wild and can be exploited so easily and to such good effect in cultivation.

One of the great advantages of these small-growing plants is that there is room for them in almost any garden. Perhaps it is the vast and elaborate rockeries of botanic gardens that, paradoxically, has led people to feel that they are not gardening on a scale grand enough to embark on growing these miniature and dwarf plants. In fact, almost any open space has room to grow a selection of rock plants combined with a few large stones arranged in such a way as to suggest their natural environment.

Working on a very small scale, a stone or imitation stone sink can be planted with an appropriate selection of really miniature alpines and rock plants and placed to form a focal point in a paved yard. Even without a special area being devoted to them, alpines and rock plants can be fitted in to many gardens, improving features that might otherwise be bare or weedy.

Perhaps more than anything else, gardeners are discouraged from planting alpines and rock plants in the mistaken belief that they are difficult to grow. Not surprisingly, there are some, among the high alpine plants in particular, that justify their reputation for being pernickety. To the enthusiast, they are probably the most exciting plants to grow, giving enormous satisfaction when cultivated to perfection. The ordinary gardener, however, wants adaptable, attractive plants that do not require specialist experience and close attention in order to be grown well.

The range of beautiful and easy plants suitable for rock gardens is truly vast, showing a great variety of foliage and flowers and with representatives from around the world. For many of the most desirable, the basic requirements are no more than free-draining soil, a sunny position and an adequate supply of water. The most common rock garden plants are much less troublesome than, for instance, the majority of popular border plants.

Coping with Latin names

One of the consequences of having such a wide range of plants to chose from is that you will encounter more Latin names than with most groups of garden plants, because many of them do not have familiar common names.

The scientific name, which is recognized internationally, normally consists of two parts and is printed in italics. The first is the name of the plant's genus – the group of closely related plants to which it belongs. It is rather like a surname and is always written with a capital letter. The second part, which does not have a capital, is the name of the species – the group of plants that, in all important respects, are the same. To take an example, the scientific name of the common snowdrop is *Galanthus nivalis*: *Galanthus* is the generic name of all snowdrops; *nivalis* is the specific name applied to all snowdrops having the botanical characteristics of the common snowdrop.

Sometimes naturally occurring varieties of a species are given an additional name. For instance, *G. n. reginae-olgae* is a naturally occurring, autumn-flowering variety of *Galanthus nivalis*. Cultivated forms of species are also given additional names, which are not italicized and are placed within quote marks. *G. n.* 'Atkinsii', for example, is a vigorous cultivated form of the common snowdrop. Note that, where there is no possibility of confusion, the generic and specific names are abbreviated to initials.

One further convention of the scientific naming of plants is that the symbol '×' is used to indicate that a plant is a hybrid (a cross between two or more species or, more rarely, genera).

Opposite *On banks like these, numerous plants thrive at the water's edge and provide a sheltered, but natural, setting for the display of many different rock plants.*

CHAPTER 1
CONSTRUCTING A ROCK GARDEN

Planning your rock garden can be great fun, but careful thought needs to be given to how big it's going to be, the site and what stones and soil are going to be used.

To build a rock garden from scratch may strike you at first as a truly ambitious undertaking. It is certainly not something to be embarked on at a whim, without considering fully the budget you can work to, the suitability of a site, the availability of materials, and the kind of help you can reasonably expect from family or friends. However, it is not a job of construction that requires vast financial resources, an unusual site, materials that are difficult to obtain, or advanced building techniques. In fact, there are many other tasks about the garden or the home that require much more sophisticated do-it-yourself skills.

Provided you are reasonably fit, or have the assistance of someone who is, and you are patient enough to set about the job methodically, there is no reason why you cannot build, at modest expense, the sort of small rock garden that will fit happily in many small to medium-sized gardens.

Choosing a site
It is not likely that the average suburban garden is going to have the absolutely ideal site for a rock garden but there are a few basic requirements on which there is limited room for compromise.

Many alpines and rock garden plants are sun-lovers, doing best in positions where they have full sun for at least half the day. While it would be perfectly possible to assemble an interesting collection of dwarf plants that flourish in shade or part shade, it would hardly be worth building a rock garden to accommodate them. They would probably look very much better in a raised bed, preferably one of peat or sod blocks.

For a rock garden, it is always best to provide a south-facing, sunny position. This will almost certainly mean an open area not overhung by trees, which also overcomes the problems of shade and drip from overhead branches and a heavy fall of dead leaves in autumn. If dead leaves are left on the rock garden they encourage

pests and disease, and small plants completely covered by them may be lost. Some shelter is desirable but this is best provided by a background of shrubs giving protection from the prevailing wind.

Although a sloping site has advantages, a level site is perfectly satisfactory, for a slight southward inclination can be created in the construction. What is much more important than the slope of the site is that it is one with adequate drainage.

You should aim to convey an impression of plants growing in their natural environment. The impression of naturalness will be diminished if the rock garden is closely associated with formal elements of the garden. However, if your space is limited, the best position may be against a wall or at the corner of two walls. Do not, though, build against the outside wall of a house because the dampproof course will almost certainly be bridged, and the scale of the building will be out of proportion to that of your miniature landscape.

One further and not negligible consideration to bear in mind when selecting a site is its accessibility. The basic materials of which a rock garden is constructed are heavy and can be awkward to maneuver. Firm and reasonably level access will make the job that much easier.

Designing a small rock garden
Before deciding on the layout of your rock garden, it is worth looking at the ways other gardeners have achieved a natural effect. Even a much larger rock garden than the one you have in mind can be a useful source of ideas but any scheme inspired by a large garden must be tailored to the space you have available.

A serious mistake you may sometimes find in suburban gardens is a rock structure of many tiers built on a relatively small base. It is as though someone has tried to miniaturize a mountain rather than suggest a rocky outcrop. Inevitably, such a structure

Opposite When building a rockery, the choice of stones will make the difference between success and failure. A few large boulders will look much more natural than many smaller ones.

looks totally unnatural. Furthermore, it requires an unnecessary amount of the most expensive component, rock, and it places emphasis on the wrong element of the garden, the stones of which it is made, rather than the plants growing in it. If you are building on a small scale, an arrangement of two tiers of large rock gives as much height as is necessary and allows for treatment of the stone as natural layers.

Another error that gardeners sometimes make is to devise a layout that is too regular or geometrical. If the surroundings impose a regular form, it would almost certainly be better to build a raised bed of the appropriate shape rather than a rock garden. For the latter, a useful outline to work to is an irregular, blunt wedge shape, the mound having a jagged profile sloping to the south.

Before beginning any construction work, mark out the outline using rope or string and pegs, fixing in your mind's eye the volume that your rock garden will occupy.

Rock to build with

There are few gardeners fortunate enough to have available on their own site sufficient rock of adequate size to make a worthwhile rock garden. For one reason or another you may have a large stock of old bricks or of cut stone. Do not be tempted to use these as a substitute for natural stone in the construction of a rock garden that is intended to look like a small, natural landscape. They will be perfectly satisfactory as materials for constructing a raised bed in which rock plants can be grown most successfully, but they will never combine with plants to create an impression of a rocky outcrop as found in nature.

Buying the rock

Rock, regrettably, is an expensive material to purchase, largely because the cost of transporting it is so high. The more local the source of the rock you buy the less expensive it is likely to be. You may find in your own area quarries or stone suppliers

Above *Choice of rock will partly depend on where you live: locally quarried stone is generally the cheapest available and will fit in with the surroundings.*

Right *A newly-built rock garden made of relatively small stones. In a year or two it will be flourishing with a fine display of plants.*

conserve moisture and discourage weeds. Use limestone chippings if you are building with limestone, but do not mix with other kinds of rock.

Improving the soil

Provided it is reasonably fertile and weed-free, ordinary garden soil to which is added sharp sand and leaf-mold or fine grade peat moss can be used to provide the earth core of the rock garden. The soil you excavate when establishing a foundation for the rock garden may be of good enough quality to form the loamy constituent but the quantity may be insufficient.

If you have to add compost, a good mixture consists of two parts of good loam to one part of well-rotted leaf-mold or fine grade peat moss and one part of sharp sand (all parts by volume, not by weight). It is important that the sand is really gritty so that it gives the mixture the open, free-draining texture that most rock plants require. The soft sand used by builders should never be used in the mixture. The components need to be mixed together thoroughly. In the process, add a general, slow-acting fertilizer (bone-meal is very suitable).

Preparing the site

Before excavating a base for the rock garden, ensure that both the site you have marked out, and the surrounding area, are free of perennial weeds, such as bindweed and couch grass. If these are not eliminated before construction begins they will become firmly established among rocks and will be almost impossible to eradicate without dismantling the structure (although there is now a selective weedkiller that will kill grasses among rock plants).

Once the site is free of such weeds, excavate the marked area to a depth of about 6in (15cm), taking off the turf first, if you are building on the site of a lawn. The

Top left *When buying your garden rock you may have to decide on sandstone or limestone and choose your plants accordingly.*

Top *Peat can be incorporated as a soil conditioner and will greatly improve clay soils.*

Above *Organic material such as farmyard manure will supply essential nutrients as well as improving the texture of the soil.*

that will sell to you direct; the larger garden centers are an alternative source of supply.

Much of the rock available falls into one of two broad categories: the sandstones and the limestones. If you want to include lime-haters, such as dwarf rhododendrons, heathers and soldanellas, you should choose a porous but not soft sandstone, preferably of a kind that is local (a consideration based not only on cost but also on the desirability of using stone that looks as though it belongs to a particular location).

If the soil of your garden is limy, the case for choosing a local limestone is very strong. You will not be able to grow acid-loving plants but you will have a rock garden that is in keeping with the rest of your garden.

Tufa, an unusual type of limestone that is porous and very light, is remarkable in that many acid-loving plants can be grown in it very successfully. Because it is so soft it is easily drilled; small alpines that are plugged into drilled holes root readily and flourish.

Marble and granite are the least satisfactory types of rock to build with. Their hard surfaces and non-porous textures are somewhat less sympathetic to plants.

Once you have chosen the type of rock you are going to use, do not mix it with rocks of another type. To do so will destroy the effect of naturalness you want to create. Although you need some variation in rock size, the larger individual pieces are (provided that they are not so heavy that they cannot be maneuverd) the better the effect they will create. In any event, no rock should be smaller than half the size of the largest piece.

A minimum quantity of rock for a small garden of about 15 sq ft (4 sq m) is in the order of 3 cu ft (1 cu m). A reputable supplier will be able to give sound advice on quantities needed for large gardens.

When ordering rock, also get a supply of chippings or pea-sized stones, to dress the surface of the rock garden and help

Left *Preparation for the rock garden is extremely important. All weeds should be removed before construction begins.*

1. *The rockery should be built to a roughly wedge-shaped pattern. Try to choose a well-drained site, preferably on a slight grad.*

2. *Once you have marked out the position of the rockery, dig out the foundations to a depth of 6in (15cm). Compact the soil firmly in the hole.*

3. *Prepare the bedding material near the edge of the hole. Mix one part grit to five parts topsoil and refill to still below ground level.*

4. *Move the largest 'key' stone into position first. Pack the soil firmly underneath to hold it securely in the right place.*

5. *Complete the L-shaped outcrop with two lines of closely packed stones that are all tilting slightly backwards and pack soil around them.*

6. *Once the lower outcrop is complete, fill the inside with bedding mix. Rake the mix out and tread it flat – do not disturb the positioned stones.*

turf will be useful if you are intending to build a sump to give your garden extra drainage. Keep them, in any event, as they can be used for repairs to other parts of the lawn.

If the excavated soil is of good quality, it can be used as the loamy constituent of your rock garden mixture. Poor quality soil is useless and will have to be disposed of completely.

Under normal circumstances, when you have excavated to the necessary depth, compact the soil in the floor of the hole by trampling it down. This will give the rock garden a stable bed and there will be little likelihood of it sinking later on.

If there is any danger of the natural drainage on your site being inadequate, before compacting the foundation provide additional drainage in the form of a sump. For a small to medium-sized rock garden the sump should consist of a centrally placed hole about 12in (30cm) square by 18in (45cm) deep filled with well-firmed gravel. The gravel can then be covered with turf that has been turned grass-side down,

or a layer of marsh hay to prevent the soil mixture working its way down into the sump and clogging it up. This layer of turf or hay needs to be firmed down, as does the rest of the floor of the hole.

Putting rock and soil together

Before moving any stone, make sure that you have the necessary equipment. You will probably possess basic garden tools, such as spade, shovel, fork and, perhaps, pickaxe. You may also find it useful to rent two crowbars (with these you will need blocks of wood to use as fulcrums and wedges) and the sort of two-wheeled "truck" that is used in warehouses to move sacks about. If you are using such a truck, it will pay to lay down planking over any soft ground between your pile of rock and the rock garden site.

If you are building on a medium-to-large scale and using a lot of really heavy stones, an arrangement of planks and rollers may provide the easiest method of moving rocks about. Rocks are levered one at a time onto a plank that is sitting, temporarily wedged,

5

6

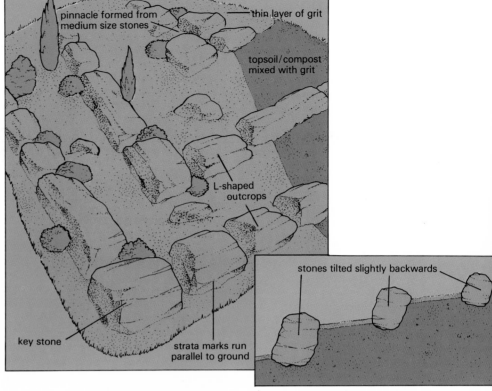

pinnacle formed from medium size stones

thin layer of grit

topsoil/compost mixed with grit

L-shaped outcrops

key stone

strata marks run parallel to ground

stones tilted slightly backwards

on five or six rollers, which are themselves sitting evenly spaced and parallel to each other on firm planks. Once the rock is securely on the top plank the wedges can be removed and the whole top plank with rock on board can be pushed along on the rollers, each roller being moved to the front as it is exposed by the plank moving forward.

Whatever method you adopt for moving rock, remember to work steadily and patiently. Accidents can happen but almost always because commonsense has been defeated by impatience. As an added precaution, wear really stout boots and a pair of working gloves.

Positioning the stones
The first stone to be positioned, the key stone, will determine the way the rest of the rock garden is built up. It should be the largest rock that you have available and, therefore, you must decide before laying it where the high point of your first tier ought to be. In many pieces of rock you can see quite clearly a layered pattern of the strata lines. To create a natural effect in the rock

garden, the strata lines should all run more or less horizontally and the weathered side of the rock should face out. If rock is not laid with the strata running horizontally, quite apart from creating an unnatural appearance, there may be a risk of water and frost penetration, which may result in the rock breaking up.

Place the key rock, bearing in mind the direction of the strata, in such a way that it tilts slightly backwards. The tilt will cause rainwater to run back into the earth behind it. The rock must be really firmly bedded in so that it is absolutely stable, even when someone stands on it. Take time to get this first stone properly positioned, packing soil around the base to get it sitting right.

Once the key stone is in place, choose a smaller stone to butt against it. To create a rock garden that is really sound structurally, it is important that one stone is pushed hard against another to form a close joint. Sometimes, of course, the irregular shape of a rock will make gaps unavoidable. Such gaps can be plugged with smaller pieces of stone wedged from behind so that soil is not washed out. However, small gaps between rocks can often be just the position to suit the kind of plant that, in its natural environment, would be found lodged in a crevice. While most planting in the rock garden is better left until after the soil mixture has settled down, it may be much easier to put in some of the crevice-loving plants during construction; at this stage it is much easier to ensure that their roots are

Above *The rockery is built on a shallow foundation filled with a carefully graded mix of grit and a good topsoil. Stones are then placed on top and formed into a number of L-shaped rocky outcrops one above the other with planting terraces in between. To aid drainage (inset) each stone should be positioned so that it tilts slightly backwards at an angle of about 15 degrees.*

7. *Construct the second outcrop in the same way as the first.*

8. *The final outcrop should consist of a few medium-sized stones formed into a small pinnacle.*

9. *Finally, cover all the exposed soil with a 1in (25mm) layer of clean grit to keep down weeds.*

10. *After a few weeks when the rockery has settled down you can start putting in the plants. When planting, turn the pot upside down grasp the stem and pull gently out.*

11. *Firm in the soil around the plant, cover with grit, and then water adequately.*

7

8

9

10

not simply packed into a hole but are worked through into soil that can sustain the plant.

As you continue to lay the stones of the first layer, step back after positioning each one to make sure you are happy with the impression you are creating. Adjustments will be so much more difficult to make at a later stage. Aim for an unforced irregularity, with some stones jutting out in front of others and, perhaps, some slight variation in the progression towards smaller stones.

11

Adding the soil

Once you have completed laying the stones of the first layer, shovel in the soil mixture to within 2in (5cm) of the top of the rocks. Make sure that soil is well worked in at the back of the stones. For the second tier begin, as before, with the largest rock and create the impression of an outcrop with a loosely L-shaped grouping. Follow the same approach as with the first tier, repeating the angled position of the rocks and ensuring that they are firmly bedded into the mixture and fitting tightly against one another. When all the rocks are in place, add the soil mixture to the second level, so that it comes to within 2in (5cm) of the top of the rocks.

The temptation will now be very strong to set about planting immediately but you should allow a good two or three weeks for the soil to settle. Only after planting should the layer of chips be added, when it should be spread over the surface to a depth of 1in (2.5cm). Work the small stones right round the necks of plants.

A sloping site

The scheme as outlined here for combining rocks and soil to make an attractive, natural-looking home for dwarf plants can be modified in many ways to suit the size and position of your own site. If you are lucky enough to have a gently sloping site, you will probably have much greater room for flexibility than if you only have a flat area. For instance, it may then be perfectly appropriate to extend to three or even more tiers of rock, which can be arranged in roughly semi-circular outcrops. Bed the rocks, always with a backward tilt, well in and keep the pockets of soil nearly level. If soil slopes too steeply, there is the danger of erosion and the whole rock garden being put at risk.

The larger garden

Where you have space for a rock garden on a larger scale, it is even more important to use stones of good size. The impression created by a few well-placed rocks will be very much more natural than clusters of insignificant stones.

In the medium or large-scale rock garden it is well worth considering a pool. The availability of flexible synthetic pool liners and fiberglass shapes has greatly simplified the addition of this feature to the garden. What is important is that, if a pool is to be incorporated in a rock garden, it adds to the impression of a natural landscape and that it does not appear as a foreign and jarring element. Planning its position and excavating for it should be done at an early stage.

The rock garden surroundings

Relating the rock garden to its surroundings can present problems for there must not be an abrupt transition from informal to formal. There are, furthermore, disadvantages in having a lawn running right up to the rock garden. It makes for difficult mowing and there is a tendency for grasses to work themselves up between the rocks. One of the most satisfactory solutions is to surround the rock garden with an edge of stone chips or gravel and paving. The ideal would be paving of the same stone as has been used in the construction of the rock garden. In any event, the paving stones should be laid in such a way as to form an edge with the lawn and allow for easy mowing of the grass.

One way of softening the base of the rock garden is to position a few tufted or clump-forming plants so that they grow against the bottom tier of rocks. Planting the paved and gravelled edge will further enhance the impression of naturalness.

Left *An ideal way of setting a rock garden into its surrounds is to edge it with paving stones of a similar material. They also go well around pools or ponds.*

CHAPTER 2
ALPINES WITHOUT A ROCK GARDEN

Building a traditional rock garden may not always be practical. Filling a raised or scree bed or possibly a miniature garden with colorful dwarf plants might well be the answer.

Although there is a particular pleasure in growing alpines and rock plants in a manner that suggests a wild, rocky landscape, there are many dwarf plants that can be a great asset in a garden where no attempt has been, or perhaps, can be made, to simulate a natural environment. In fact there are many circumstances in which the construction of a rock garden would be an unwarranted labor.

Raised beds

In a small garden the raised bed offers the most attractive alternative to the rock garden as a way of growing alpines and other small plants. Indeed, many gardeners would claim that the raised bed has many advantages over the rock garden itself. One of its principal advantages is that, while it needs to be sited, as the rock garden does, in an open but sheltered and reasonably sunny position, it can be co-ordinated very readily with formal or informal settings. Furthermore, the range of materials that can be used satisfactorily in its construction is very wide. This may mean that if you have available, say, a supply of old bricks, the materials for construction need not be an expensive item. One very attractive advantage that the raised bed has for anyone who is partially disabled is that, once constructed, it makes a particularly easy garden to maintain. Even from a wheelchair, it is possible to do most or all of the work that will keep a raised bed in good condition.

Constructing a raised bed

In essence, a raised bed consists of suitable free-draining soil raised to a height of anything between 6in (15cm) and 30in (75cm) by low walls of any stable material. In practice, most raised beds are built to a height of about 24in (60cm) and to a width, rarely more than 5ft (1.5m), that allows the whole surface to be reached from one side or the other. A raised bed can be of almost any shape, including circular, curved, rectangular or L-shaped. What is important is that it fits comfortably into the space that you have available for it.

Among the materials most commonly used in construction are stone and artificial stone, bricks and railroad ties. Whatever the material, a fundamental requirement is that the walls are absolutely firm and stable. Constructing with bricks and mortar, for instance, may require greater building skills of you than are called for in the erection of a small rock garden, but there are other materials that pose few problems. One of the most satisfactory results is achieved with dry stone walls, which allow many possibilities for rock plants to be grown so that they hang down the rock face.

Although each of the materials requires a different treatment in construction, you must always start with a firm, weed-free base that has good drainage. Make sure that, in addition to good drainage at the base, there are drainage holes in the retaining walls near ground level.

Once the walls have been constructed, put in a bottom layer up to 6in (15cm) deep of rubble and firm it down. It is a good idea to cover this with gravel to a depth of 2in (5cm) before putting in the soil mixture. As for the rock garden, the soil mix should consist of a well-blended mixture two parts loam, one part well-rotted leaf-mold or fine grade peat moss, and one part of sharp sand (all parts by volume) to which has been added a slow-acting general fertilizer. Fill the bed to within 2in (5cm) of its top with the mixture and then allow to settle over a period of several weeks before planting.

Break up the surface of a raised bed with one or two medium-sized stones jutting out in a natural-looking way. They will help to give substance to the bed in the quieter months of the year and, more importantly, they will provide the cool root run from which so many alpine plants benefit.

Opposite Raised beds can be constructed in most garden locations and have the great advantage of being extremely easy to maintain.

Choosing plants

The plants that are grown in raised beds are much the same as those grown in rock gardens. Particularly where the construction is of dry stone, there is plenty of accommodation for those plants that do best wedged in the crevice of a near-vertical face. Once planting is completed, cover the whole surface of the bed with a 2in (5cm) layer of some stone chip, of limestone if your soil is limy, otherwise of a neutral or acid type of rock.

"Peat" beds

An interesting variant of the raised bed, the peat bed, while not strictly speaking a rock garden, provides an ideal way of growing a number of dwarf, plants, especially if your garden is on lime. The bed raises the plants sufficiently so that their roots do not reach the limy soil beneath. A peat bed can also be a happy solution to the problems posed by a shady garden as many acid-loving alpines tolerate shade, but a site directly under trees is not suitable. Wherever the bed is situated, the foundation should be reasonably free-draining and clear of any perennial weeds.

Constructing a peat bed

In the United States, of course, true peat beds, as they are constructed in the British Isles, are impossible since the peat blocks from which they are built are rarely, if ever, sold here. However, we can come up with a passable substitute by using blocks of a good closely-knit sod for the walls.

Before beginning construction, make the blocks moist, but not muddy. Excavate a course for the first layer of blocks so that they will be half-bedded in the ground. The sod walls can then be built to a height of about 24in (60cm). As each course is completed, fill the bed to the height of the course with a mixture of peat and lime-free soil in equal quantities by volume.

Below *Once constructed, a "peat" bed can be cultivated with as wide a variety of plants as an ordinary rock garden.*

Below right *Raised beds are ideal for growing rock plants in a confined area and the harsh edges will soon be softened by a tumbling display of flowers.*

Choosing plants

Among the lime-hating plants that flourish in the moist and acid conditions of a peat bed are the magnificent dwarf rhododendrons and numerous small herbacous plants and ferns. Growing some of the smaller plants in the peaty bed will help to knit the blocks more firmly together.

A peaty bed is easy to maintain but it should never be allowed to dry out; once thoroughly dry, peat and blocks are very difficult to wet again. Give the bed an annual top-dressing of fresh peat and a general fertilizer in early spring.

A scree garden

In a garden with a gentle slope (preferably facing south) that links two levels, it may be preferable to construct a scree bed rather than a rock garden. The gardener's scree bed is a miniature and modified version of a feature that is sometimes very extensive in mountains, where wind, rain and frost are endlessly breaking down the rock mass. In alpine screes, many plants have adapted to the growing conditions of these sometimes rather unstable accumulations of weathered, rocky debris. The requirements of these and similar plants can be satisfied without too much difficulty by the creation of this uncomplicated and extremely charming feature in the garden.

Constructing a scree bed

To construct a scree bed you need to excavate your sloping site to a depth of about 24in (60cm) and to ensure that at the base of the slope there is very free drainage. It may be necessary to lay drainage tiles that will carry water away to a lower level, but a trench some 18in (45cm) wide and deep filled with rubble will be an adequate sump in most conditions.

Use a fork to loosen the floor of the excavated area and then fill to between half and two-thirds of the excavated depth with a mixture consisting of equal parts by volume of good loam, well-rotted leaf-mold or peat, and sharp sand. The remainder should be filled with stone chips. If your soil is naturally limy, do not fight against it but reconcile yourself to the exquisite, dwarf, lime-loving and lime-tolerant plants and provide for them a covering of limestone chips.

Choosing plants

On a sloping site where the soil is naturally neutral or acidic it is perfectly possible to provide neutral or acidic conditions at the top of the slope and limy conditions at the bottom, so that plants of widely varying soil preferences can be grown.

The surface of the scree bed needs to be broken up with several rocks or groups of rocks. Many small plants seem to grow more happily when they are snuggled against a stone and certainly there are many alpines that need the kind of cool root run that a few well-placed rocks will provide.

Although the plants suitable for a scree bed demand free-draining conditions, they also require plenty of moisture in spring and summer. At these times of the year, especially in hot spells, some watering will almost certainly be necessary. A sprinkler or a hose fixed at the top of the scree will make long, thorough soaking easy; a light sprinkling of water will be of very little use.

The scree bed is not the place for boisterous tumbling plants, for these would soon swamp the little cushion plants, neat trailers and compact mat-formers that do best in these conditions. When planting in the scree bed try to get the roots down as deeply as you can so that they can quickly

Top left *A scree garden can be constructed to provide the very sharp drainage needed for some alpines.*

Above *A slightly raised bed can be made into a scree garden and provides a labor-saving feature along the path. It is colorful in the early spring and, by careful selection, can be interesting all year.*

Above *An ideal container for a miniature garden is a stone sink or trough where small alpines can be assembled permanently.*

Above right *A simple indoor miniature garden can be made in a clay seedpan, using small perennial plants from pots. The garden will be a delightful and fascinating source of interest for a long time.*

penetrate to the soil mixture beneath the chips. Especially in the early stages after planting, you will need to maintain an adequate moisture level in the stones to support the plants until they are well established. Make sure, too, that your planting includes one or two small shrubs and dwarf conifers as well as suitable herbaceous perennials.

The construction of a scree bed is a very simple matter that requires no special equipment and little heavy work. Furthermore, weeding is not a serious problem, for the deep mulch of chips discourages the growth of undesirable plants. It has to be admitted, though, that unlike the rock garden or raised bed, all work on the scree bed is at ground level so that it is not an attractive proposition for the less mobile gardener.

Miniature gardens in troughs and sinks

A really miniature alpine garden can be created very effectively in a trough or sink of quite modest dimensions. There are, in fact, any number of tiny plants of exceptional beauty that, when planted in a large setting, can easily go unobserved.

Real stone troughs have become difficult to obtain and when they are available they are generally very expensive. There is no doubt that there is something about them when planted up with alpines and dwarf rock plants that is not matched by their substitutes. A stone trough well-positioned in an open sunny part of a paved yard makes a really distinguished feature.

Making an imitation stone sink

However, an old glazed sink, preferably a deep one, can be treated to look very like stone and is far from being a poor alternative. The treatment consists of applying a rough, stone-like coating comprising one part sand, one part cement and two parts peat. Clean the sink thoroughly and remove any piping still attached. Coat the sink on the outside and to about 3in (7.5cm) inside the lip with a PVA adhesive (for this operation it will be easier if you mount the sink on blocks). When the adhesive is tacky, combine the mixture with water to get a stiff consistency and apply it to the sink. The easiest way to get a rough natural effect is to apply by hand, but wear rubber gloves. Protect the sink from weather for a few days and then leave exposed for several weeks before filling and planting.

Before adding the soil mixture or plants, place the sink or stone trough in its permanent position, an open sunny site, raised on bricks so that water can escape without difficulty from the drainage hole or holes. Take care when moving a coated sink about for, although the covering will stand up well to weathering, it is easily chipped. Except in the case of shallow sinks, fill the base with a 2in (5cm) layer of broken crocks, and in all cases make sure that the drainage hole is clear but covered so that soil will not be washed through.

The soil to use in a sink will depend on the plants you want to grow, but a standard mixture consists of two parts loam, one part leaf-mold or peat and one part of sharp

Left *A sink, or trough, garden is the perfect location for hardy, cushion-forming alpines, evergreens and also small succulents.*

sand, all by volume. Fill to within 2in (5cm) of the top and then cover the surface with a layer of stone chips. One or two pieces of rock protruding from the surface will give a natural effect. Tufa goes particularly well in trough or sink gardens and allows the flexibility for plants to be grown at more than one level.

Choosing plants

Among the many plants suitable for these delightful miniature gardens are the truly dwarf species of dianthus and campanulas as well as a great range of saxifrages and sempervivums. The dwarfest available forms of conifers can also look very much at home.

Maintaining a sink or trough garden requires very little work and, because there is little bending involved, can be a source of very great pleasure to the semi-invalid or to the fully able gardener. Watering is the one job you will need to be attentive to, as these small gardens can dry out very quickly in hot weather.

There is no room in such a tiny garden for plants that grow too big or too fast. If you find that by mistake you have introduced something that is too vigorous, make sure you are ruthless in replacing it.

Rock plants in paving and dry stone walls

Even without a purposely-built location, such as a rock garden or raised bed, there are positions in many gardens where dwarf rock plants and alpines can be grown to very good effect. The bright flowers or soft foliage of a few well-chosen plants can really transform areas of the garden that might otherwise be nondescript and appear rather boring.

Planting dry stone walls

In many gardens there are dry stone retaining walls which sadly are often left bare or are allowed to be colonized by weeds. They offer enormous scope for growing some vigorous and free-flowering rock plants.

It is very much easier to plant in a dry-stone wall during the process of construction rather than later; but even in an established wall it is possible to get plants to take. Some can be put in as seeds, mixing them with damp soil to make little pellets that you can work into the crevices.

The best way to introduce most plants, however, is to insert small rooted cuttings into cracks and crevices, pushing damp soil in around them. Inevitably, there will be failures but it only requires a few of the vigorous plants to become established and in a very short time you will have a wall that is a highly ornamental feature of the garden.

It is particularly worthwhile persevering with some of the rosette-forming plants that resent water collecting at the base of

Below left and right *A garden wall can often be an ideal place to grow some colorful dwarf rock plants and alpines.*

their leaves and are, therefore, often difficult to grow on level sites. Lewisias, for instance, are excellent plants when grown lodged in a crevice whereas in a level garden it can be difficult to give them the drainage they need. Many of the larger saxifrages also do very well grown vertically so that their handsome sprays of flowers arch out from the wall.

Planting paved areas

The softening effect of plants can seem even more important in paving than on walls. So often it is desirable to blur the edge where one part of the garden meets another and to introduce variations of color and texture to relieve a monotonous expanse of paving.

Unless there is a more general need to renovate existing paving, lifting it with the intention of improving the growing conditions for rock plants should not be undertaken lightly. Look instead for some other way of softening the surroundings. It is surprising, however, the way some plants, the thrifts, for instance, will establish themselves in the poor quality soil that lies between and underneath most existing paving. The best chance you have of establishing plants is to take out what sand and grit you can where there is a sizeable gap between paving stones and then work in a loamy mixture into which a small rooted cutting can be planted. Water frequently in the weeks immediately after planting until it is well established.

If you are laying new paving, there is much greater opportunity to allow for spaces in which rock plants can be grown. At the outset it is important to decide which paved areas are going to take a lot of traffic. These should be left without planting and with the paving materials closely fitted. Elsewhere, however, gaps can be left and soil of good quality incorporated. Among the plants suitable for growing in these little pockets are the smaller bulbs, cushion and mat-forming perennials and dwarf conifers.

It must be said, however, that the planned accommodation of rock plants in paving rarely achieves the natural effect that results from the apparently casual colonization of old paving.

An alpine lawn

For those who have the scope to garden on a more generous scale, a lawn planted with dwarf bulbs is one of the loveliest ways of recreating an alpine meadow. What must be borne in mind at the start is that such a lawn will not be cut for much of the year because the leaves of bulbs must be allowed to die down naturally. If they are cut off too soon the bulbs become progressively weaker, and flowering suffers. You must decide at the beginning that you can live with uncut grass through spring and early summer.

There will be few gardeners who have a rock garden large enough to take an alpine lawn. Almost certainly, it is better to make it a feature of its own or one that blends into a more extensive lawn. An ideal site is a sunny gently sloping piece of ground with good drainage.

Before planting, make sure that the area is free of perennial weeds. Provided that it is applied according to the manufacturer's instructions, a hormonal weedkiller used in mid-summer will leave grass undamaged but deal with broad-leaved weeds.

Bulbs should be planted at their normal times. For most, this is sometime during mid or late autumn. Remember, however, that snowdrops do best transplanted immediately after flowering. To achieve a natural effect, plant bulbs in clumps, avoiding a rigidly symmetrical arrangement. Individual bulbs can be planted by lifting out a plug of turf and soil, adding a little bit of fresh soil and the bulbs and then replacing the plug. With the really small bulbs it is enough to ease open a hole by working a trowel back and forwards in the soil but be sure that when the bulb is planted it is firmly bedded in earth and that there is no air pocket underneath it. To

Below A single specimen can be grown in a small pot where space is limited. Featured is Dionysia curviflora.

plant ten or twelve bulbs in a clump, lift a square of turf, loosen the exposed soil, and plant the group well-spaced before replacing the turf.

Crocuses, miniature daffodils, and snowdrops are obvious choices for the alpine lawn but others that do well are anemones, chionodoxas, hardy cyclamen, erythroniums and scillas. Most bulbs need to be planted at a depth of 2–3in (5–7.5cm) but *Cyclamen hederifolium* (syn. *C. neapolitanum*) and *C. coum* should have their corms only just covered by soil.

Growing in pots

The emphasis of this book rightly falls on ways of growing alpines and rock plants in ways that suggest their setting in the wild. However, many of these plants can be grown to good effect in pots and some of the choice, but difficult, dwarf alpines are best grown in this way.

Pans of sempervivums and miniature bulbs require little special attention and can be moved about in the garden to give them prominence at the most appropriate time of the year. The alpines that are more delicate in cultivation are fully hardy but suffer in relatively mild, wet winters. In their natural habitat, snow cover in winter provides insulation and keeps them comparatively dry. At lower altitudes, if exposed to wet weather, these plants are likely to rot.

Alpine houses

The principal purpose of an alpine house, in which these plants are sometimes and often successfully grown, is to provide an environment in which it is possible to control the amount of moisture these plants receive. It is also possible in the alpine house to cater to the individual requirements of more difficult plants, by adjusting the soil mixture, drainage, or exposure to light; for a few difficult plants these adjustments may tip the scales for success.

While it has to be admitted that the alpine house is for the real enthusiast, there is no doubt that it can be made into an exceptionally interesting garden feature, giving a changing display of miniature plants – dwarf bulbs, cushion-forming saxifrages, primulas, campanulas and small-growing conifers – that sustains interest throughout the year and is especially fine in winter and the early spring.

Above *Many plants grown in pans and pots in an alpine house provide a riot of bloom during the colder months of the year.*

CHAPTER 3

CHOOSING, PLANTING & CARING FOR ALPINES

Once the construction of your rock garden is complete, you can then have the fun of choosing all the different varieties of rock plants and alpines that you want to include.

Building a rock garden or whatever similar feature you have decided on is the hard work. The selection, planting and care of alpines and rock plants is almost all pleasure. Of course, it is not a matter of grabbing armfuls of plants in the garden center willy-nilly and thrusting them in with reckless abandon. That kind of gardening may work very satisfactorily with annual bedding plants but it is certainly not worth taking the trouble to construct a rock garden or raised bed if that is how you want to set about planting it. With alpines and rock plants your choice should be a matter of discrimination in which several factors are taken into account, among them the soil requirements of plants, their ultimate size and the way that they will fit into an overall scheme that has year-round interest.

Where to get your plants

You are most likely to start looking for alpines and rock garden plants at your local garden center, where there will probably be a special section devoted to perennials. However, even the choice a garden center offers is, in most cases, a relatively small range of only the commonest plants, which frequently means those that are easiest to propagate. Simply because these plants are common does not make them any less desirable, particularly as a starting point, but once you have started with a few plants you may want to try the less familiar.

Specialized nurseries

There are, fortunately, a number of first-class nurseries specializing in plants suitable for the rock garden. For most of the nurserymen involved, their business is as much a labor of love as it is a commercial enterprise. Their catalogs are a source of valuable information on the requirements of particular plants and the staff at the nursery are generous with advice when it is requested. To find the names and addresses of nurseries begin by consulting gardening magazines.

Some nurseries do not have the staff or the facilities to welcome visitors; they take orders and despatch by mail. But there are others with retail outlets at the nursery site and these are worth visiting for the ideas you can glean on the way plants are grown and for the pleasure of seeing a wide range of unusual plants in cultivation.

Gardening clubs

Do not overlook the advantages of joining a club. An encounter with a rock gardening enthusiast may lead to suggestions of ways to grow this or that, and a gift of a few rooted cuttings. Making personal contact with others who share an interest in rock garden plants is a very pleasurable way of expanding one's own knowledge of them.

By joining a society that caters to the specialized interest of the rock gardener you will be able to draw on the accumulated wisdom and experience of amateur and professional growers through casual contacts and an organized program of lectures and visits to gardens. Quite apart from the opportunities that you will have for exchanging plants, there is generally an annual distribution of members' surplus seeds organized by specialized societies. Seeds from such distributions can provide an interesting way of building up a collection of some of the less usual plants.

Testing the soil

How is one to set about choosing from the many plants that are suitable for growing in the rock garden? A first consideration must be the nature of your soil, specifically its acidity or alkalinity. The standard measure of acidity/alkalinity is the pH scale. On this, a reading of 7 is neutral, below 7 indicates acidity and above 7 alkalinity. There are simple soil-testing kits available using a liquid chemical indicator that, when mixed with a soil sample, changes color according to the acid or alkaline content. The color of

Opposite *Successful rock gardens take a lot of careful thought. The plants need to be chosen for their suitability rather than at random.*

the liquid is measured against a color chart to give an approximate pH reading. Green may indicate that the soil is neutral, red that it is acid and blue that it is alkaline.

Many plants that do well on limy, (nearly alkaline), soils can also be grown quite satisfactorily on neutral or slightly acid soils. Acid-loving plants, however, can be more precise in their requirements. Although most will tolerate a neutral soil, they will fail to thrive if put into a more alkaline soil.

Whatever limitations your soil imposes on your choice, the range of really desirable plants will still be vast and there will always be something else to try!

Remember, too, that the raised bed can be a means of providing soil conditions that are different from those at ground level. If you have more than one raised bed or trough garden it will not be difficult to have different soil conditions in each, so that you can grow plants ranging from those that flourish in acid soils to those that love lime.

Sun or shade?

The degree to which the rock garden is exposed to the sun will be another factor influencing the plants you choose and where you position them. While it is true that very many alpines and rock plants require, or at least prefer, full sun, and most rock gardens are built in an open position, there is usually room on the shady sides of rocks and walls for those dwarf plants that prefer cool, moist conditions.

The choice of plants

It is sometimes said of rock gardens that, although they are wonderfully colorful in spring and early summer, for the rest of the year they have little of interest to show. It would be remarkable if any part of the garden could sustain throughout the year the sort of performance that the rock garden puts on in spring. Nonetheless, as with other parts of the garden, there is no reason for the rock garden to be dull at any time of the year. If a garden falls short in this respect it is because the gardener has failed to exploit the full range of species and cultivated forms of dwarf plants. But the rock gardeners who achieve the most appealing results are the true plantsmen, people with a passionate love of plants in all their forms, who choose their plants with an overall scheme always in mind.

Dwarf conifers

Although the main plants of the rock garden are the dwarf herbaceous perennials, there are other categories that should be allowed to play an important role. There is sometimes a rather imprecise line dividing the herbaceous perennials and the dwarf flowering shrubs, while the dwarf conifers make a quite distinct group. These miniature versions of sometimes giant cone-bearing trees are slow-growing evergreens that look completely at home among rocks and with alpines. True, if planted to excess, they risk creating a grotesque impression, but when

Below *A rock garden constructed in an enclosed situation with a seemingly natural scree but with dwarf conifers and shrubs to break up the level effect.*

Below right *Many ferns will thrive in the conditions provided by a rock garden and are well suited to the shady areas around large outcrops.*

Left *The elegant drooping fronds of a well-placed fern contrast with the texture of the rock behind.*

Above *Miniature bulbs provide a welcome burst of color and* Iris histroides *'Lady Strawley's Form' flowers early in the year.*

planted judiciously they are enormously valuable for giving a green backbone to the rock garden or raised bed.

The word 'green' is far from adequate to describe the considerable variations of color among conifers – there are shades of silver, blue-gray, reddish-brown, and gold. Their scale and rate of growth are also far from uniform. While some will reach a height of 3ft (1m) in about 12 years, there are others that are so tiny and slow-growing they can be planted in a sink garden. Another characteristic to take advantage of is the wide variation in habit. Many forms are pyramidal or conical in shape, while others are prostrate or columnar; some have very upright growth, while others have a weeping habit. It is not difficult to make a selection of dwarf conifers that, far from being a desperate arrangement to ensure that the rock garden is clothed at all times of the year, brings into it a group of plants that are very desirable in their own right.

Miniature bulbs

While dwarf conifers are the evergreen mainstay of the rock garden, it is the miniature bulbs that provide the most colorful element in autumn, late winter and early spring. They are not plants to be dotted about, for then their effect is lost. They make their greatest impact when planted as groups according to kind. Then it is as if the garden is lit by a series of minute, timed explosions beginning in the shortest days of the year. It is hard to praise too highly the virtues of the early spring bulbs, which, for all the appearance of fragile beauty, are astonishingly robust and capable of standing up to the worst weather of the year. However, they are plants whose merits are widely recognized.

The hardy dwarf cyclamen, on the other hand, although greatly appreciated by many keen gardeners, are still not as widely grown as their qualities deserve. Between them, the species give a very long flowering season, extending well into the grim winter months. Their pretty shuttlecock flowers stand up well to rough weather and the leaves, which are marvellously patterned in silvery green, are a long-lasting bonus in the winter months. To complete their list of virtues, some are sweetly scented and most are very easy to grow. No rock garden should be without them.

Ferns and grasses

Two other groups of plants that are often unnecessarily neglected are the ferns and grasses. In the rock garden, as in the large-scale garden, variations of texture and form can be as important in giving interest as brightly colored flowers. Foliage plants with linear or bold, deeply divided leaves can make striking contrasts set against rock or other leaves. Ferns are far from being plants exclusively of dank and dark places, but they are particularly useful for planting on the shaded walls of raised beds.

Replacing plants

The choice of plants should not be thought of as something that, once done, has been done for good. There will be outright failures and plants that fail to thrive in one position but flourish when moved somewhere else. Many rock plants and alpines are long-lived and those that are not tend to self-seed freely. However, from time to time you will need to replace old plantings with freshly propagated material or with completely new stock. Experimenting with the range of plants available to the rock gardener is an inexhaustible source of pleasure.

Planting

The main planting period for the herbaceous perennial and shrubby alpines and rock plants is between the early and mid-spring. However, because stock is available from rock garden nurseries pot-grown, the gardener has great freedom in choosing the time to plant. What must be avoided in the autumn-spring period is planting when the ground is frosted or snow-covered. At other times of the year, the problem is to ensure that the plant has adequate moisture. It is easy to lose specimens if you are unable to keep them watered when there is a dry spell.

When choosing where to position individual plants, you must try to bear in mind your overall scheme while at the same time meeting their special requirements. Sequences of flowering and contrast of form and color are important considerations but in allowing for them do not forget to leave plenty of room for vigorous, spreading plants. Keep them well away from your choice miniatures, which might otherwise be swamped.

If your garden is an established one with a layer of chips on the surface, brush these back before digging a hole with a small trowel (one with a narrow blade is particularly useful in the rock garden). The hole must be large enough to take the root-ball but not so large that the plant, once in the ground, will sit any deeper than it does in the pot. There is a risk of plants succumbing to rot if they are put in too deeply. At this stage, you have the chance to make slight modifications to the soil to suit more precisely the requirements of individual plants: peat can be incorporated for those preferring a moisture-retentive soil and additional grit can be worked in for those types of plants needing particularly sharp drainage.

To remove a plant from its pot, place two fingers on the surface of the soil, one either

Right *Early and mid-spring are the best times for planting alpines, but you must make sure that the ground is not frosted. The saxifrages featured can be planted when they are in flower.*

side of the plant, then turn the pot upside down and tap it to free the soil ball; the pot can then be pulled away. If the plant has started to become pot-bound, loosen the roots slightly before dropping the plant into its hole. However, it is much better to avoid buying pot-bound stock; when you are buying, inspect the underside of the pot and do not take plants with roots that can be seen to be growing noticeably through the drainage holes.

Once the plant is in the ground, check that it is at the right depth, adding or taking away soil in the bottom of the hole if necessary and then fill round it before firming in. If the plant is not well firmed in, there will be moisture loss, the roots will not spread readily into the soil of the rock garden, and there is the danger that wind will further loosen the plant. Finish by spreading chips over the surface of the soil, working them well up to the base of all the plants.

Planting in crevices

Planting in crevices, as has been suggested, is most successfully done at appropriate stages in the construction of the rock garden. In the established rock garden or dry stone wall the problem is to ensure that the roots have enough moisture-retentive

soil about them to connect with the body of soil behind the rocks. Planting between stones is most successfully done in the autumn to mid-spring period using small, rooted cuttings. Work in as much soil underneath and above the plant as you can and, in the case of a vertical crevice, trickle in some chippings so that you completely cover the soil.

Transplanting

If mature plants need transplanting, this, too, should be done in the early to mid-spring period. Pay particular attention to firming the soil around the plant; the easiest way may be to tread it in with the feet.

Bulbs

Unlike the herbaceous and shrubby plants, bulbs have a limited planting season. Dry bulbs should usually be planted mid to late autumn, the sooner the better, except for tulips, which, to reduce the risk of a disease called tulip fire, are planted in late autumn. Snowdrops become established more readily when planted 'in the green', in the period just after flowering, than as dry bulbs. Some specialized nurseries offer them at this time and it is certainly the moment to choose if you are transplanting your own stock.

As everywhere in the garden, bulbs look best planted in groups. The miniatures, in particular, lose their effect if dotted about. Bulbs can be dropped into individual holes but it is generally easier to dig out a hole to a depth of 2–3in (5–7.5cm), large enough to take a clump of five or six bulbs. If the species or variety requires particularly sharp drainage, the bulbs can be bedded in a layer of coarse sand.

Planting in pots

For pot cultivation of perennials and shrubs as well as bulbs, ensure that there is good drainage by placing a layer of crocks in the bottom of the pot. Make sure that the drainage holes are not blocked but are

Below *Bulbs are most effective when planted in groups – here a cluster of miniature tulips add a blaze of color.*

Bottom and bottom left *Many rock plants look good and grow well in the crevices between stones. Dianthus (bottom) contrasts well with the soft sandstone of the rock work.*

Above *Lack of rainfall in a rock garden can be made up by watering or by using artificial sprinklers that provide a gentle supply of water over a long period.*

Right *A well-cared for rock garden will require little attention through the year, though wooded locations will need tending in the autumn months. Fallen leaves should be gathered up regularly.*

sufficiently covered so that the compost is not washed out. The soil mixture can be very finely adjusted to suit the requirements of the plants you are growing but, for many, it will not be necessary to vary a standard mix of two parts loam to one part coarse sand and one part peat or leaf-mold (all parts by volume). The surface of the soil mix should be covered with a layer of fine chips or gravel.

With bulbs, it is possible to get a really striking display by planting two layers to a pan. The bulbs of the first layer are covered to their necks with the mixture and the bulbs of the second layer are then set above them.

Caring for rock garden and alpine plants
A rock garden with a well-balanced soil covered with a mulch of stone chips is unlikely to need much attention apart from routine maintenance, throughout the year.

Watering
In periods of prolonged drought, a thorough soaking will be necessary every two or three days. If possible, apply as a fine mist with a sprinkler. Small raised beds, including those made of sod blocks, scree gardens and sink gardens, will probably need watering more frequently during warm dry weather than does a simple rock garden. Do not delay watering until plants show signs of flagging, for by then the damage may have been done. You will quickly get a feel for the water needs of whatever feature you have.

In an alpine house, some form of automatic watering will save a lot of work. A common practice is to bed the pans of plants in trays of gravel into which there is a controlled flow of water.

In winter, excess water will be a problem with some of the rock garden plants with most interesting foliage. Those with woolly, felted and hairy leaves are prone to rot in long spells of wet weather during the dormant season. The solution is to provide a shelter that will keep off excess rain but will allow light to reach the plant and a free circulation of air. This is easily done with small panes of glass held above the plants by wire supports. These will probably need to be in place from late autumn to early spring; and it must be admitted that they will detract from the overall impression of the rock garden as a small piece of natural landscape.

Collecting leaves
Many rock garden plants are liable to rotting if buried under accumulations of dead leaves. From winter through to early spring, collect and dispose of any leaves that gather. As well as encouraging the development of destructive molds, piles of dead leaves provide lurking places for slugs, the most destructive pest in the rock garden. It is, therefore, worth clearing all debris away as a frequent routine job.

Weeding
Weeding, too, should be treated as a routine activity. The mulch of stone chips on the surface of the rock garden will do much to discourage the growth of weeds but inevitably there will be some that will take root. Annual weeds, such as chickweed and groundsel, develop quickly and, as a rule, are prodigious seeders. They must be uprooted long before their seed has had a chance to set and been dispersed about the garden. Perennial weeds including bindweed and similar plants, are so vigorous and tenacious that they can pose a threat to the viability of a rock garden once firmly established. All weeds compete with plants for nutriments and moisture.

The use of a hoe is not advisable in the rock garden as you are likely to cause damage to the roots of plants. Instead use a small hand fork to loosen weeds before pulling them out and disposing of them.

Chemical weedkillers are rather difficult to control in the rock garden but it may be necessary to use an appropriate proprietary brand if perennial weeds are difficult to remove physically. With some it may even be necessary to paint the weedkiller onto the leaves.

Weeds are easily introduced to the garden lodged among the roots of new plants that have been bought or received from friends. Always check new stock to make sure that you are not introducing an unwelcome or serious nuisance.

Top-dressing
The plants in the rock garden do not need a rich soil but will benefit from an annual top-dressing. A suitable mixture consists of two parts loam to equal parts coarse sand and peat or leaf-mold to which has been added a slow-acting fertilizer such as bone-meal. Do one section of the rock garden at a time, sweeping the rock chips to one side before applying the top-dressing. Then return the stone chips to the surface, topping it with new chips if necessary. The top-dressing should be worked in among the leaves and branches of dense mat-forming plants.

Pruning
Most rock garden plants do not need to be pruned or trimmed but the exceptions include some of the most popular and easily

Below *All the plants in the rock garden will benefit from an annual top-dressing of fertilizer. The rock chips should be removed before the dressing is added and replaced afterwards.*

grown. Alyssum, aubrietas and saponarias, for instance, benefit from being cut back as soon as flowering is over. If left untrimmed they become loose and untidy. Cutting them back will keep the growth compact and in some cases may encourage a later flowering the same year. Some vigorous sprawlers may need trimming, too, simply to prevent them engulfing other less robust plants. Plants that become untidy and loose at the center will benefit from being lifted and divided every two or three years, the worn-out center being discarded. Divide plants in the dormant period, before growth in early spring.

Propagation

For the beginner and the experienced gardener alike there are few greater pleasures in gardening than that derived from managing the processes by which plants increase themselves. There is a very special pleasure in looking on a collection of plants that you have raised from seed or from cuttings and brought to maturity. It is a satisfaction that in some ways is out of proportion to the role the gardener plays – with so many plants there is little that needs to be done to encourage the reproductive process. For the gardener with a new rock garden or raised bed, it would require pointlessly stoic patience to raise all plants from seed or cuttings and it would mean a rather bare rock garden for at least a season. Once the first planting has been done, however, it is well worth trying your hand at a fascinating and economic way of increasing your stock.

Raising plants from seed

The most straightforward way of increasing your stock is to raise plants from seed. However, many cultivated varieties of plants will not come true when raised from seed and, where closely related plants are grown near to one another, there is the likelihood of hybridization.

The seeds of plants vary considerably in size and in the length of time that they take to germinate. In the case of many alpines, seed only germinates freely after being subjected to a period of sharp cold. Generally, it is not until early spring that seed becomes available for sowing but it is often better to sow fresh seed at the end of summer or in early autumn.

Many sorts of containers are now used for raising plants from seed but, for alpines, clay pots are still preferred by most gardeners. Before using them for new sowings, clean them thoroughly and then place a crock over the drainage hole or holes so that the soil mix is not easily washed out. The soil mix should be soil-

based rather than peat-based; the most satisfactory mixture for most plants will be a fairly fertile one to which has been added about half as much again by volume of coarse sand or grit. Remember that the mixture for lime-hating plants must be neutral or acidic. When the mixture has been firmed down it should come within ¾in (18mm) of the pot's rim.

Sow the seeds thinly and evenly on the firmed surface. It is easier to distribute very fine seeds evenly if they are mixed with a little dry sand and shaken onto the surface from a folded piece of paper. The seeds need to be pressed lightly into the soil mix before a thin layer of the same is sprinkled on top. At this stage, stand the pot in a basin of water until the surface darkens to show that water has been taken up.

Complete the job by adding a thin layer of grit over the surface, then label. The gritty layer reduces the risk of seeds being washed out in heavy rain and prevents the surface becoming compacted. Make sure that the labelling is durable for the seeds can take more than a year to germinate.

The pots need to be placed in a cool, lightly shaded position until the seeds germinate. The ideal is an open frame with a bed of coarse sand into which the pots can be sunk, for this will help maintain an even level of moisture.

Keep an eye on the pots; as soon as the first true pair of leaves show, the seedlings should be pricked out and potted up, either individually or with several to a larger container (with enough space for the roots to develop without being cramped). A suitable mixture for this consists of a fairly good soil to which has been thoroughly mixed one part peat and one part grit. Before the roots have filled the container, sturdy specimens should be planted in their permanent positions.

Division

The simplest method of vegetative propagation is by division. Perennial rock plants with fibrous roots can be lifted before growth begins in early spring and divided into several pieces. Only vigorous, well-rooted pieces should be kept; old woody and straggly material should be discarded. The vigorous portions, which should be put in immediately, give instant new plants. Division of herbaceous perennials is an important part of the cycle of renewal in the garden.

With bulbous plants, division consists of lifting established clumps in the dormant summer months and separating the offsets from the main bulbs. The offsets can then be planted up individually and brought on until they are of flowering size.

Below *All newly propagated plants should be carefully labelled to avoid confusion when the time comes to set them in a permanent position.*

Cuttings

Propagation from cuttings is another vegetative method of increasing stock. It is the commonest way of reproducing the cultivated forms that would not come true if grown from seed. There are two major types of cutting that are relevant to rock garden and alpine plants. The first are soft, fresh stems taken early in the summer. Healthy, non-flowering stems about 1in (2.5cm) long should be cut just below a leaf or a pair of leaves. The lower leaves are then removed.

The second main type is again of young growth but firmer. The cutting is taken with a heel (a piece) of older wood by tearing the stem sharply downwards.

Hormonal powders and liquids, generally containing fungicides to inhibit the growth of molds, are commonly used now to promote rooting but they are far from being indispensable. Whether you use them or not, insert the cuttings up to their leaves round the edge of pots containing an equal mixture of peat and coarse sand. The cuttings need to be kept in a warm, humid environment but out of direct sunlight. As with seedlings, a useful way of maintaining an even humidity and temperature is to plunge the pots in a bed of sand or grit inside a frame.

Cuttings need to be watched closely; any that show signs of wilting or mold should be removed immediately. When they have rooted, they should be potted up individually using a mixture consisting of a fairly good potting soil to which has also been added one part peat and one part grit.

Layering

This technique of vegetative propagation calls for patience but it is useful as a means of increasing woody plants that are difficult to propagate from cuttings.

The technique consists of choosing a flexible, young branch that can be bent down to the ground. Here, it is pegged down in soil to which peat and sharp sand have been added. Before fixing the branch in position, make a cut on the underside of the stem about 1–2in (2.5–5cm) long so that it passes through a joint. This is the part that must be kept in the soil with the cut kept open, for instance by lodging a small pebble in it. An application of hormonal rooting powder or liquid at the cut may speed up the process of root formation. The stem must be held securely in position with a rock or brick and the end of the stem should be staked in as near an upright position as possible.

It may take a year or 18 months for a layer to develop an adequate root system that will allow it to be severed completely from the parent shrub.

Left When you are housing small cuttings of rock plants in cold frames, some ventilation must be given during the day in the winter months. Condensation and a stagnant atmosphere encourage damping off.

Below Growing cuttings inside a frame can be very successful as they get the humidity and temperature necessary to develop.

CHAPTER 4

WHAT CAN GO WRONG

Rock plants and alpines are naturally quite hardy plants but from time to time they can be troubled by pests and diseases. Easy preventative measures can be taken to reduce these risks.

The point has already been made that rock garden plants are remarkably trouble-free, provided that their basic growing requirements are satisfied. From time to time, however, there will be problems with pests and diseases, but the damage can be limited by taking preventative measures and dealing promptly with attacks when they occur.

Pests
Like almost all garden plants, alpines can be attacked by various pests and, unless action is taken to safeguard them, some much-loved favorites may be lost.

Slugs and snails
The most troublesome pests in the rock garden are the slugs and snails. They have a particular passion for some of the choice alpines, including the dwarf campanulas, and can make devastating raids on mild, humid evenings.

The use of a stone mulch on the rock garden will go some way to discouraging the movement of slugs and snails, and the removal of all debris, particularly dead leaves, will reduce the number of areas that could harbor these pests. A reasonably effective protection can be achieved by laying proprietary slug baits. For instance, particularly vulnerable plants can be surrounded by a ring of slug pellets. These will need to be renewed at reasonably frequent intervals in the critical period of spring and early summer. It is difficult to devise a method of keeping rain off pellets that is not unsightly but it may be feasible to prop up a piece of slate relatively inconspicuously and place the pellets underneath this.

Birds and animals
After slugs, birds are probably the greatest cause of damage to rock garden and alpine plants. They can be a great test of one's good-natured acceptance of wildlife in the garden; at some times of the year, one being during early spring especially, their activities are little short of vandalism. The plants that suffer most are the rosette and cushion-forming alpines, which can be set

upon and torn about until there is very little left to salvage. Sparrows may also vandalize early spring bulbs, energetically pulling apart yellow crocuses particularly.

Sparrows

Mice

Again, the problem is to find a way of discouraging their activities that is not unsightly and, frankly, it is a problem not easily resolved. Cones of mesh can be put over highly valued plants but this is certainly not an inconspicuous solution. Perhaps the best approach is to use a crisscross web of black thread supported on sticks just above the flowering plants.

Mice can also be a problem, especially with young rock plants. Rodent repellent, however, can be sprayed on the plants.

Aphids
In the main, garden aphids are among the most troublesome pests, sapping plants of their strength and often transmitting serious viral diseases. These pests reproduce at a phenomenal rate so that they form quaking black, pink or greenish clusters on any sappy growth. Although many rock garden and alpine plants are too thrifty to be appetizing to aphids, new growth will sometimes be attacked. Infestations should be dealt with promptly. The most convenient treatment is to spray with a systemic insecticide.

Caterpillars
Some other pests will occasionally cause minor problems. For example, caterpillars

Green aphids

Caterpillar

may eat leaves or flowers. If there is leaf damage and there are no silvery trails as slugs or snails would leave, then caterpillars are likely to be the culprits. Proprietary sprays can be used to deal with them but the best solution is to search among the leaves, particularly in the center of plants, and remove the pests by hand. If you go out with a torch at night you will probably find them fully active.

Ants
If ants build nests around the roots of plants this can cause water loss. With cushion plants, for example, the appearance of brown patches may be a clue to this problem. Proprietary ant killers are available and these should be used around the plant according to the manufacturer's instructions.

Diseases
While there are numerous diseases that can attack the various plants that are grown in the rock garden, there are very few that affect a large range of plants, and surprisingly few that, in the ordinary course of events, the gardener has to worry about.

Grey mold
Grey mold (botrytis) is a fungal disease that can cause serious damage in damp weather. It is a fungal infection that shows as grey woolly patches on parts of leaves and stems that have darkened. Plants with hairy or felted foliage are especially vulnerable in the winter months and it is for this reason that they are sometimes protected from excess moisture with panes of glass.

In the alpine house an outbreak of gray mold suggests that ventilation is inadequate. One has to remember that the purpose of an alpine house is not to provide a necessary warmer, snugger environment than outdoors, but one where it is possible to control the amount of moisture that reaches plants, with a free movement of air.

Gray mold can be treated by spraying with fungicides, the systemic kinds are probably the best to use, but in the case of a seriously debilitated plant the best course is to take it out and burn it. It is sometimes tempting to persist but a plant that has been seriously attacked can be a source of infection for the rest of your collection.

Viruses
The same ruthless approach is advisable when plants are suffering from viral attacks. These are not common in the rock garden but occasionally plants show distorted growth and abnormal streaking and mottling of foliage. There is no way of treating viral infections, so plants suffering from them should be dug up and burned.

Other disorders
If you have tested your soil properly and chosen your plants well, it is unlikely that you will have planted a lime-hating plant, such as a rhododendron, in soil that is alkaline. However, if leaves on an acid-loving plant turn yellow between the veins, it is likely that the soil is too limy. The best course may be to lift the plant and grow it in a pot with an appropriately acidic soil. An alternative to try first is to incorporate peat, which is normally strongly acidic, around the plant and to apply a proprietary chemical compound (chelated iron) that will help to correct the chlorosis caused by the lime.

There are other mineral deficiencies that may cause yellowing leaves and, for instance, the symptoms of manganese, magnesium and nitrogen deficiencies may be difficult to distinguish. Treatment for these problems involves spraying or feeding with appropriate chemicals – manganese sulphate for manganese deficiency, magnesium sulphate for magnesium deficiency, and for lack of nitrogen a nitrogenous fertilizer. If you are not sure what the problem is, try spraying with a foliar food containing trace elements as well as major nutrients.

One other problem that is sometimes encountered in the rock garden is damage to buds when they thaw too rapidly, after a frost. This can mar the beauty of early-flowering rhododendrons planted in open positions where early-morning sun reaches them. If it is a problem, it is worth repositioning plants so the sun touches them later in the day and frost, therefore, has a chance to thaw slowly.

Slug

Below *Soil can easily be tested with a kit and any acidity that is found can be quickly corrected.*

CHAPTER 5
ROCK GARDEN CALENDAR

Planning the plants of your rock garden should always be done on a seasonal basis to keep the right balance of flowering and evergreen plants throughout the year.

Early spring

The flowers of the first weeks of spring are probably more eagerly anticipated than those of any other season of the year. It is the moment above all others for the dwarf bulbs to bring life to the rock garden, but there are strong splashes of color from easy perennials, such as the aubrietas.

Jobs to do

Clear away dead leaves and other debris that might harbor pests and diseases. The dead leaves attached to herbaceous perennials can now be cut down.

Weed and, if not yet done, loosen the soil with a small hand fork, taking care not to damage roots.

Apply a top-dressing, which, for the majority of plants, should consist of two parts of loam and equal parts of coarse sand and peat (all by bulk) to which has been added a dusting of bone-meal. After top-dressing renew the mulch of stone chips.

Firm plants and labels that have been lifted by frost, and make a check of plants that have been lost over the winter.

Plant out own-raised stock grown on from the previous year or new stock as soon as it becomes available. Label at planting time.

Propagation by division of deciduous

and evergreen perennials should be completed promptly. If snowdrops need lifting and dividing, this should be done as soon as flowers die. Sow seeds indoors and prick out all the seedlings when they develop.

Clean and put away glass panes that have been used to keep excess moisture off hairy and felted plants throughout the winter months.

Plants to enjoy

Alyssum, Androsace, Chionodoxa, Crocus, Daphne, Erythronium, Galanthus, Iris, Muscari, Narcissus, Primula, Saxifraga.

Mid-spring

The small bulbs continue to play an important role during this season but at last the rock garden begins to look more clothed with green. From now until early summer the dwarf rhododendrons are among the most conspicuous of the flowering shrubs.

Spring-flowering gentians.

Jobs to do

Continue weeding and complete forking the surface and top-dressing.

Planting should be finished as soon as possible to allow plants to become fully established before the warmer, drier weather of summer puts them to the test. It is the best time of the year to plant dwarf conifers, which are beautiful plants in

A rock garden in the spring.

their own right and useful as major components in the design of a rock garden. Water in all new stock thoroughly and label clearly.

Sow seeds of rock plants and prick out seedlings as they develop. As the weather becomes warmer, the seed pans will dry out more quickly. Do not water from overhead but stand the pan in a basin of water and let it take up moisture until the surface darkens.

Cut back trailing stems of early-flowering perennials, such as aubrieta and alyssum, as they finish flowering. This keeps the plants compact and shapely.

Plants to enjoy

Alyssum, Androsace, Arabis, Aubrieta, Cytisus, Erythronium, Gentiana, Leucojum, Muscari, Narcissus, Primula.

Crocus tomasinianus.

Late spring

Late spring is without doubt one of the loveliest periods of the year in the rock garden for it is a time when the last of the spring bulbs combine with a number of free-flowering perennial and shrubby rock plants to give a really full display.

Alyssum saxatile *and Aubrieta.*

Jobs to do

Pests, encouraged by the milder weather and new growth, will multiply rapidly. The most troublesome are likely to be aphids; the best method of control is to spray with a systemic insecticide, repeating regularly about every ten days. Ants, too, can sometimes be a nuisance, tunnelling among the roots of plants. Use a proprietary powder sprinkled around the nest holes if there is serious damage. Although more isolated, devastating pest damage in the rock garden can be caused by slugs, which are active in warm and

Ants can be a problem.

moist weather. To protect vulnerable plants, lay slug pellets in their vicinity.

Weeds will be encouraged by warm moist weather. Check them before they have a chance to seed.

Check seeds. Continue to watch seed pans closely, and prick out seedlings as soon as they have become large enough to handle successfully.

Propagation. At this time of the year many plants can be propagated from cuttings of new, soft growth. Insert in pans of a sandy mixture, cover with a pane of glass or clear plastic, and keep moist.

Plants to enjoy

Aethionema, Achillea, Aquilegia, Armeria, Aubrieta, Campanula, Cytisus, Dryas, Genista, Gentiana, Geum, Gypsophila, Iberis, Phlox, Potentilla, Pulsatilla, Rhododendron, Scilla, Tulipa, Veronica, Viola.

Early summer

The fullness of late spring continues into early summer, with the alpine pinks and the campanulas among the most conspicuous plants.

Jobs to do

Watering may be necessary if there are long spells of dry weather. Do it in the afternoons so the plants can dry off. Apply in a fine spray.

Pest control is still important. Continue

to use a systemic insecticide primarily against aphids and similar sucking pests. From time to time change the insecticide used so that pests do not build up a resistance to a particular chemical.

Collect seedheads of the less common alpines and rock plants, throughout the summer and the autumn. Sowing seed as soon as it is ripe is likely to produce good results. In this way you will be able to maintain and increase your own stocks of a desirable plant and have material to exchange with other gardeners for uncommon plants you do not yet have. Germination of some species can be very slow, so mark pans of seed carefully.

Continue to take soft cuttings and start taking cuttings of older wood with a heel.

Cut back trailing plants that have finished flowering, to encourage compact growth. In some cases this may induce a second crop of flowers in late summer.

Dwarf rhododendrons should have dead heads removed to encourage a good crop of flowers next year.

Plants to enjoy

Achillea, Alchemilla, Allium, Androsace, Aquilegia, Aster, Aubrieta, Dianthus, Genista, Geranium, Geum, Helianthemum, Gypsophila, Hebe, Hypericum, Iberis, Leontopodium, Papaver, Phlox, Sedum, Rhododendron, Veronica, Viola.

Remove dead flowerheads from rhododendrons to help future flowering.

Mid-summer

Throughout this season there are still many plants in flower in the rock garden but the flush of late spring and early summer is over.

Jobs to do

Continue weeding. It is particularly important to get rid of weeds before they seed.

Aphids may still be a problem so maintain a program of spraying against them.

Clip back trailing plants as they go over.

Water if prolonged dry weather persists. Give a thorough soaking every two or three days rather than a light watering more frequently. Pay particular attention to sink gardens, which are very prone to drying out in hot, rainless weather.

Continue to collect seed of choice plants, clean it and sow as soon as ripe.

Propagate suitable plants from softwood and heel cuttings.

When lifted bulbs can be kept in a box.

Bulbs that need to be lifted should be taken up as their leaves die down. Most can be replanted immediately but store tulip bulbs in the warm (but not hot), dry conditions until autumn.

Plants to enjoy

Alyssum, Dianthus, Campanula, Gentiana, Geranium, Hebe, Helianthemum, Hypericum, Phlox, Penstemon, Potentilla, Sedum, Sempervivum, Viola.

Late summer

At the end of summer the rock garden can seem rather short of flowering plants. This is a good moment to review your whole planting scheme and to consider what should be added by way of late-flowering and long-flowering plants, and those with interesting foliage and shape throughout the year. Take the opportunity of looking at other gardens to see what late-season plants there are and consult the catalogues of specialized firms. Get orders in early for autumn delivery.

Jobs to do

Plant bulbs as they become available; purchases should be made without delay. Except for tulips, the sooner bulbs are planted the better. Avoid dotting single bulbs here and there but plant in clusters.

Top *A rock garden in the late summer.*

Above *Azalea cuttings can be taken in the month of August.*

Lift and divide bulbs if necessary. Small offsets can be potted up to be brought on to flowering size.

Continue to take cuttings, ensuring in particular that you root replacement stock for short-lived plants and those that have become tired and straggly. It is a good time to take heel cuttings of the dwarf rhododendrons. Rooting is often easier if some soil from where the plants grow is added to the rooting medium.

Plants to enjoy

Alyssum, Cyclamen, Gentiana, Oenothera, Papaver, Potentilla, Viola.

Left Saxifraga oppositifolia latina.

Early autumn

As elsewhere in the garden, the range of plants now in flower is very much reduced. There are, however, some plants of real quality that give the garden a lift at this time. They include dwarf cyclamen, autumn-flowering crocuses and some of the Asiatic gentians.

Jobs to do

Tidy up the rock garden, clearing away leaves and debris. Keep an eye out for attacks of mold, which can be dealt with using a fungicidal spray.
Sow freshly gathered seed. Many alpines will germinate freely provided the sown seed is exposed to frost during winter.
Take dwarf conifer cuttings.
Finish planting bulbs other than tulips.
Plant shrubby and herbaceous rock plants. New stock should be well watered in and clearly labelled. As mid-autumn approaches plants can be lifted and divided. Some evergreen shrubs can be satisfactorily transplanted at this time of the year.
Begin construction of a new rock garden or raised bed. Ensure that basic preparation, including the elimination of perennial weeds, is thorough.

Plants to enjoy

Acer, conifers, Crocus, Cyclamen, Gentiana.

Below *Dwarf conifer cuttings.*

Below right *Protect hairy plants in the winter with sheets of glass.*

Mid-autumn

This may prove a stormy period, with a lot of rain and spells of cold weather.

Take what opportunities you can to tidy up the rock garden so that it is well in order before winter.

Jobs to do

Clear away dead leaves; if they are left lying damp on rock garden plants they may cause rotting. In addition, they provide a cover for slugs, which can be active at this time of the year.
Protect plants with woolly or hairy leaves grown in the open. They may need protection from excess water in the winter

Left *Tidy up the rock garden in mid-autumn.*

months, and this can be done by fixing small panes of glass on wire frames over individual plants.
Continue planting herbaceous and shrubby perennials if it is not too frosty.
Divide established plants.
Continue with the construction of new rock gardens and raised beds if the weather is dry. Some planting, particularly in rock crevices, is more easily done during construction than later. In

A two-pronged fork is good for planting.

general, however, it is advisable to allow a period of settling before planting, which can be carried out in the spring.
A stone or imitation stone sink can now be planted.

Plants to enjoy

Acer, conifers, Cyclamen, Gentiana.

Late autumn

There is still a little flower color in the autumn rock garden, particularly from the hardy dwarf cyclamen. However, from now until winter, the principal interest will be in the foliage of evergreens such as the dwarf conifers. Some of these take on new interest at this time of year, turning bronze or deeper shades of blue-gray. Examine your rock garden in the winter months to see if the look of it might be improved by the addition of dwarf evergreens.

Jobs to do

Check for weeds and self-sown seedlings. Some plants self-seed so prodigally that fairly drastic thinning is desirable.

Remove dead leaves from the rock garden. Check over the plants at least once a week.

Plant tulips. Other dwarf bulbs should have been planted by early autumn but now is the time to put in tulips.

Plant deciduous shrubs in mild weather. Many established deciduous shrubs can now be transplanted safely.

Herbaceous perennials can still be planted in good weather in mild areas.

Plants to enjoy

Conifers, Cyclamen, Erica, Galanthus, Gentiana.

Early winter

There is probably no period of the year when there is less happening in the garden. Yet the rock garden need not be without interest. The varied ericas, for instance, which may flower right through until early spring in mild areas, are colorful and attractive little plants that are well worth using in moderation to brighten the rock garden during the winter months.

Jobs to do

Remove dead leaves promptly during regular checks on the rock garden.

Birds can be a considerable nuisance during the next few months. In cold spells they may attack small plants, particularly choice rosette and cushion-forming kinds, and pull them to pieces. The vandalism can be devastating. There is no simple solution that is entirely satisfactory, but one method of discouraging attacks is to tie black thread on sticks to form a criss-cross net a little above (about an inch) over vulnerable plants. Another good method is to cover single plants or groups with small cones of chicken wire.

Plants to enjoy

Conifers, Cyclamen, Erica.

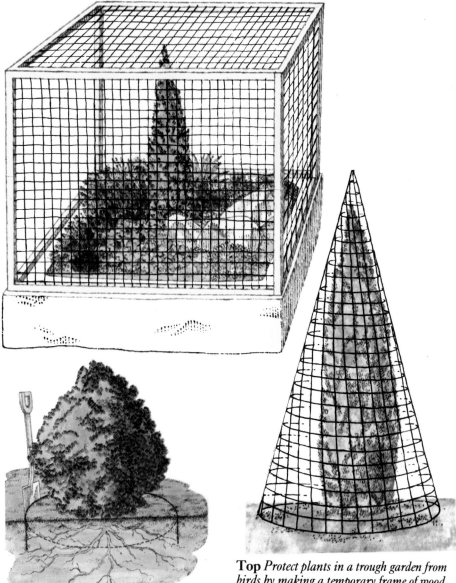

Mid-winter

Although mid- and late winter are the coldest periods of the year, and many plants are still dormant, there is, at times a sense of growth getting under way. The shoots of dwarf bulbs may start to show and some of the most precocious begin to flower even while snow is on the ground in sheltered places.

Jobs to do

Slugs can still be a problem during mild spells. Ensure that dead leaves are cleared away and continue to apply slug pellets.

Dislodge heavy falls of snow that have accumulated on the branches of shrubs.

Continue with the planting of herbaceous perennials and deciduous shrubs in fair weather.

Seeds are often sent out by specialized gardening societies at this time of the year. Sow alpines as soon as received.

Take root cuttings of plants that can be

Top *Protect plants in a trough garden from birds by making a temporary frame of wood covered with chicken netting.*

Above *Protect plants in the rock garden with cones or wigwams of chicken netting.*

Left *Evergreen shrubs can be transplanted in late autumn.*

propagated in this way.

Avoid construction work in wet weather. If, however, the surface of the ground is very frozen, this is a good opportunity to move rocks or some soil mix about.

Plants to enjoy

Conifers, Crocus, Cyclamen, Erica, Galanthus, Iris, Saxifraga.

Late winter

Nowhere in the garden is there a more dramatic foretaste of the advent of spring than in the rock garden. The growth rhythm of dwarf bulbs begins to pick up speed despite spells of cold bleak weather, and the aubrietas may break into full flower particularly in sheltered spots.

Jobs to do

Clear away debris accumulated over winter and set about weeding the rock garden in a methodical way, clearing a small section at a time. The sooner weeds are dealt with the less work they will make. Start going over the rock garden with a small hand fork loosening the soil but avoiding any damage to the roots of cultivated plants.

Apply a top-dressing consisting of two parts of loam and equal parts of coarse sand and peat (all by bulk) in which a dusting of bonemeal has been incorporated.

Remove the dead rosettes of plants such as saxifrages, and work stone chips into the gaps.

Dress the rock garden with chips. Use limestone for lime-tolerant plants, granite for lime-haters. This will help conserve moisture and suppress weeds.

Sow alpines and rock garden plants as soon as the seeds become available.

Plants to enjoy

Aubrieta, Chinodoxa, Crocus, Daphne, Erythronium, Galanthus, Iris, Muscari, Narcissus, Primula, Saxifraga, Scilla.

Left and below *A rock garden during the winter months.*

Bottom Galanthus nivalis 'Flore Pleno', *the double form of the snowdrop.*

CHAPTER 6

PLANT GUIDE

There are numerous varieties of plants available for your rock garden. This guide contains a comprehensive selection to add interest and color to all types of garden.

This chapter contains an alphabetical list of plants that you might want to grow. It is not exhaustive and you may well find other species and varieties, especially in specialized nurseries, but the plants included here will provide plenty of interest throughout the year . . . and there are plants to suit every situation in the rock garden.

In some cases, the nomenclature is confused because on the one hand botanists are prone to change names as new research comes to light and, on the other, the plants distributed through the trade may not be botanically correct. Where this is likely to lead to particular confusion this has been pointed out, but generally the plants are listed under the names used commercially.

Most of the plants are available from garden centres or from specialized alpine plant nurseries, but you will find some are difficult to obtain even from specialists. They may, however, be available from seed, or even through seed exchanges among members of specialized societies – a good way to obtain some of the rarer kinds.

Abies *see* Conifers.

Acer

The slow-growing maples are among the best-suited deciduous small trees to introduce to the larger rock garden or raised bed. Mature plants will reach over 10ft (3m), with matching spread, but it is worth growing them even if they have to be discarded when they become too large. They are plants of exceptionally beautiful foliage, as lovely in spring and summer as they are in autumn, when the leaves take on vivid coloring.

A. japonicum 'Aureum', 3ft (1m), has lime-yellow leaves throughout summer, turning bright red in autumn.

A. palmatum 'Dissectum', 3ft (1m), forms an elegant mound of finely divided, light green foliage.

A. palmatum 'Dissectum Atropurpureum', 3ft (1m), is like the former except that the leaves are a deep purplish-red, making a particularly good foil for lighter colors.

Cultivation: Plant acers in sheltered positions (the leaves can be damaged by cold winds or frosts) in moisture-retentive soil that is neutral or acid. Reputable nurseries will supply named forms grafted onto appropriate root-stocks. Propagation of maples from seed is possible but germination can be erratic and named forms will not come true.

Achillea

The achilleas, popularly known as yarrows or milfoils, were named after the Greek hero Achilles, who is said to have used the leaves as a dressing for his wounds. The dwarf achilleas are admirable and easy rock garden plants. The fern-like leaves form attractive silvery mats above which the flat flower heads are borne over a long period throughout the summer. The fragrance can be rather pungent.

A. clavennae, 6in (15cm), has finely cut, bright, silvery foliage and pure white flowers.

A. × 'King Edward', 6in (15cm), is an excellent hybrid, forming tufts of gray-green foliage and producing sulphur-yellow flower heads.

A. tomentosa, 6in (15cm), a plant with downy, gray-green leaves, makes dense heads of deep yellow flowers.

Cultivation: Grow in any ordinary, well-drained soil in full sun. Plants can be grown from seed sown in spring or early summer. Division is an easy method of propagation and is advisable every two or three years, if plants are to be kept neat.

Adiantum

The maidenhair ferns are commonly grown as indoor plants but one species that is readily available is fully hardy and suitable for planting in rock gardens.

A. sedatum, 12in (30cm), is a deciduous species with dainty fronds and a rhizomatous root. In winter the dead fronds are attractively colored.

Cultivation: Plant in well-drained (but not too dry) soil in the light shade. The easiest method of propagation for this plant is by the division method.

Opposite *There are many hundreds of rock plants and alpines to choose from, with a wide selection for all locations. Most rhododendrons, for example, are excellent for acid soil.*

Right Androsace lanuginosa *is one of the easiest rock jasmines to grow and its delicate pink blooms make a fine summer display.*

Below Aethionema *'Warley Rose' is a hardy evergreen popular for its long flowering season.*

Aethionema

The stonecresses are evergreen trailing plants which, in their native Mediterranean region, are found in sunny, dry conditions. They are useful in the rock garden for the long season, from late spring well into summer, during which they produce a profusion of candytuft-like flowers.

A. grandiflorum, 12in (30cm), makes a spreading plant with gray-green leaves and a lasting display of delicate, pink flowers.

A. pulchellum, 6in (15cm), is similar to *A. grandiflorum* but on a smaller scale. The pink of the flowers is more intense.

A. 'Warley Rose', 6in (15cm), has wiry stems and blue-gray leaves that make an attractive background for the pink flowers.

Cultivation: Aethionemas prefer an limy soil but in this respect are not unduly fussy provided they have good drainage and full sun. The hybrid *A.* × 'Warley Rose' can only be increased from cuttings but the species can be raised from seed.

Allium

The dwarf ornamental members of the onion family include a number of attractive bulbs suitable for planting among herbaceous and shrubby rock garden plants. Some of them have showy flowers and they are useful for carrying the bulb season on into summer.

A. amabile, 6in (15cm), a plant with a rhizomatous root, is neat and small enough to be grown in a sink garden. In late summer there are loose heads of two to six purplish flowers.

A. beesianum, 10in (25cm), is a rhizomatous species, which in midsummer produces heads of pendant white and blue flowers.

A. cyaneum, 6in (15cm), rhizomatous, is a tufty plant of narrow leaves that in midsummer bears erect, deep blue flowers.

A. narcissiflorum, 8in (20cm), rhizomatous, is one of the loveliest of the dwarf alliums. The hanging bell-like flowers, which can vary in color from pink to plum, appear in mid-summer.

A. oreophilum (syn. *A. ostrowskianum*), 6in (15cm), a bulbous species with narrow leaves. In summer it produces heads up to 2in (5cm) across and consisting of numerous purple-pink flowers.

Cultivation: Plant in any well-drained soil in a sunny position. The bulbous species benefit from drying out after flowering. Alliums can be propagated from seed, which sets readily, and by splitting bulb clumps or division of rhizomes.

Alyssum

The alyssums, as their common name madwort suggests, were once thought to cure madness. They include a number of dwarf species that are easy and showy plants for the rock garden.

A. montanum, 6in (15cm), makes a loosely spreading plant with gray-green leaves. The yellow flowers are borne in late spring and early summer.

A. saxatile, 6–12in (15–30cm), the commonest rock garden alyssum, may spread up to 18in (45cm). The dense heads of bright yellow flowers make a fine display from mid-spring to early summer. Among named forms 'Citrinum', with pale yellow flowers, and 'Plenum', a rich yellow double form, are particularly desirable.

Cultivation: Alyssums tolerate a wide range of soils but should be planted in a dry position in full sun. They can be grown very successfully on walls and banks. After flowering, trim plants to prevent them becoming straggly. Plants are easily raised from seed. They can also be propagated by division or from cuttings which have been taken early in the summer.

Androsace

The androsaces, or rock jasmines, are essentially alpines. Some are among the choicest plants for the alpine enthusiast but their cultivation can be difficult. However, there are some species that are not too demanding and these can be grown satisfactorily in the scree bed or rock garden provided there is very good drainage.

A. carnea, 1–3in (2.5–7.5cm), makes a tight cushion of small leaves, that in early to mid-summer, is covered with pink primula-like flowers.

A. lanuginosa, 3in (7.5cm), has a trailing habit and is a useful plant for planting in a crevice. The silvery leaves make a pretty foil for the pink flowers, which are borne in the late summer months.

A. primuloides (syn. *A. sarmentosa*), 4in (10cm), is probably the easiest to grow of the androsaces and makes small, dense rosettes from which the pink flowers emerge in late spring. A number of different named forms are available.

Cultivation: Plant androsaces in full sun in soil that is freely draining and preferably containing limestone grit. Some overhead protection from excess moisture may be advisable in winter. Plants can be propagated from seed, from cuttings, or by division in spring.

Anemone

Among the anemones, or windflowers, are a number of dwarf species that are easy and attractive plants for the rock garden. When planted in numbers and allowed to naturalize, they make vivid splashes of color in spring. Those listed are all plants with rhizomes or tubers.

A. apennina, 6in (15cm), has fern-like leaves and flowers similar to those of *A. blanda* in pink, blue, or white that come out in early to mid-spring.

A. blanda, 6in (15cm), one of the loveliest and best known of the spring-flowering anemones. The flowers are normally blue but there are also other excellent named forms that are deep blue, pink and white in color.

A. coronaria, 6–12in (15–30cm), is one of the parents of the De Caen and St Brigid anemones. Though these large-flowered hybrids generally look out of place in the rock garden, the true species, which has white, red, or blue flowers, is a plant well worth growing.

Cultivation: These spring-flowering anemones do well in most well-drained soils in full sun or light shade. Plant the tubers or rhizomes in autumn. Stock can be increased from offsets or by division of the rhizomes when the top growth has died down in summer.

Antennaria

Among the antennarias only one species and its forms is commonly cultivated as a rock garden plant.

A. dioica, 4in (10cm), is a mat-forming plant of silvery foliage spreading as much as 18in (45cm). The small heads of white flowers tinged pink are borne in late spring and early summer. The form 'Minima' is more compact, while 'Rosea' has deep pink flowers.

Cultivation: These plants are easily pleased if given a sunny position in well-drained soil. They do well planted in paving and, in the rock garden, make an effective planting associated with vigorous small bulbs.

Aquilegia

The dwarf columbines are flowers of late spring and early summer, as lovely for their foliage as they are for the distinctive spurred flowers.

A. alpina, 12in (30cm), has gray-green leaves and has large blue or blue and white flowers.

A. bertolonii, 4in (10cm), is a lovely plant for the rock garden, rich blue flowers being borne over a tuft of very attractive blue-green leaves.

Cultivation: The columbines listed are not difficult plants and will do well in sunny or lightly shaded positions. Individual plants are not long-lived but stocks are more than maintained by self-seeding. *A. alpina* is, in fact, too generous a seeder to plant among choice plants. Where different species of columbine are grown together they will hybridize freely and pure stock will be difficult to maintain.

Top *One of the best-known alyssums is* A. saxatile *'Citrinum', its showy lemon-yellow blossom has earned it the popular name of Gold Dust.*

Above Anemone blanda *is an excellent spring-flowering anemone available in many different colors.*

Arabis

The common snow-in-summer *(A. albida,* syn *A. caucasica)* grows too vigorously for it to have a place in the rock garden but there are related plants that are more amenable.

A. ferdinandi-coburgii, 'Variegata', 3in (7.5cm), forms mats of variegated foliage that are prettier than the white flowers.
Cultivation: The plants listed need well-drained, gritty soil and positions in full sun.

Arenaria

The arenarias are not showy plants but they are useful mat-forming creepers.

A. balearica, 1in (3cm), forms mats of bright green leaves spreading as much as 18in (45cm) and starred with white flowers in late spring and early summer.

A. montana, 3in (7.5cm), makes a mat of deep green leaves with a spread up to 18in (45cm). In early summer it produces a profusion of glistening white flowers.

A. purpurascens, 2in (5cm), a prostrate plant making a mat some 12in (30cm) across, and bearing purplish flowers in the summer months.
Cultivation: Arenarias should be planted in well-drained soil. *A. balearica* needs a shady position. *A. montana* tolerates part shade but it and *A. purpurascens* do well in full sun. Plants can be propagated by division and, in the case of *A. montana,* from cuttings taken in summer.

Armeria

The common thrift *(A. maritima)* is one of the conspicuous wild plants of rugged ground by the seashore. It and its relatives are thoroughly at home in the rock garden and they are among the plants that can be introduced very effectively between slabs of paving.

A. caespitosa, (syn *A. juniperifolia),* 3in (7.5cm), is a really miniature alpine that is suitable for a small sink garden. The flowers are normally pink. The selected form 'Bevan's Variety' has deep coloring.

A. maritima, 8in (20cm), despite being such a familiar plant (the common thrift) is well worth a place in the garden. Selected forms are very desirable. These include: 'Alba', white; 'Bloodstone', deep red; 'Merlin', deep pink; and 'Vindictive', red.
Cultivation: Any free-draining soil and sunny position will suit these plants well. They can be grown from seed planted in spring and can be propagated by division and from cuttings.

Right *'Beechwood' is a lovely, colorful form of* Aster alpinus.

Below Asplenium adiantoides, *a spleenwort, is a reliable and hardy fern.*

Opposite *(top) Justifiably popular, aubrietas are one of the most widely-grown rock plants.*
(below) Blechnum spicant, *the european hard fern or deer fern, a plant for a shady part of the rock garden.*

Artemisia

This large genus includes a number of plants with elegant, finely cut leaves that are of greater interest than the flowers. Most are too large for the rock garden but two at least are well worth a place.

A. lanata (syn. *A. pedemontana*), 6in (30cm), is an evergreen cushion-forming plant with delicately cut grayish leaves. Yellow flowers are borne from mid-summer until early autumn.

A. schmidtiana 'Nana', 3in (7.5cm), makes a soft feathery clump of silvery leaves. The inconspicuous yellow flowers are borne at the end of summer.

Cultivation: Artemisias like a light soil and plenty of sun. Some protection from excessive moisture in winter is advisable. Plants are most easily increased from semi-hardwood cuttings.

Asplenium

The spleenworts are a group of more or less evergreen ferns that includes a number of hardy dwarf species particularly suitable for the rock garden.

A. adiantoides, 4in (10cm), makes black-stemmed clumps of leathery and very glossy leaves.

A. ruta-muraria, 4in (10cm), the wall rue, is a remarkably tough rhizomatous plant of creeping growth.

A. trichomanes, 4in (10cm), the maiden spleenwort, is a pretty, lime-loving species with wiry stems and colorful, bright green rounded leaflets.

Cultivation: Plant in damp weather during the growing season, working plants into crevices with a gritty compost to which peat or leaf mold has been added. Propagate by the division method.

Aster

Among the asters are several dwarf species suitable for the rock garden that make a handsome show of daisy flowers.

A. alpinus, 6in (15cm), is a native of the European Alps. It forms spreading clumps of gray-green leaves and in late spring bears orange-centerd flowers, which can vary in color from pale mauve to purple. Selected forms include 'Beechwood', bluish-purple, and 'Wargrave Variety', pink with darker shading.

Cultivation: These are easy plants for well-drained sunny positions. Divide and replant every two or three years otherwise clumps become untidy and the plants less vigorous in growth.

Aubrieta

There are probably no rock garden plants more widely grown than the aubrietas. In spring they give a long and bold display of

vivid color with little effort required of the gardener. However, they are not plants to associate with choice subjects, which they will quickly swamp.

A. deltoidea, 4in (10cm), spread 24in (60cm), is now represented in cultivation by numerous selected forms, which range in flower color from pale pink to plum and mauve to deep blue. Choose plants when they are in flower to be certain of selecting good color forms.

Cultivation: Any open, sunny position in the rock garden or in a wall is suitable. Cut back after flowering to keep growth neat. Although plants are easily raised from seed, selected forms must be increased by division or from individual cuttings.

Blechnum

The two species of this fern listed here are evergreen perennials that are useful in the rock garden.

B. penna-marina, 3in (7.5cm), is a creeping plant forming mats of dark green leaves.

B. spicant, 12in (30cm), an acid-loving fern, is like a larger form of *B. penna-marina*. Many of the curiously crested sporets this species has produced have been maintained in cultivation.

Cultivation: Grow in well-drained soil to which peat or leaf mold has been added. Partial shade is preferable. Propagate by the division method.

of mid-green leaves during a long season that starts in mid-summer. Flowers come in many shades of blue and there is a lovely white form.

C. garganica, 4in (10cm), a good wall plant, bears masses of starry blue flowers in late summer. The form 'W. H. Paine' has dark blue flowers with white centres.

C. portenschlagiana (syn. *C. muralis*), 4in (10cm), a trailing plant that does well in a shady wall, makes a bold display of starry blue flowers in late summer. However, it is a vigorous spreader that should not be introduced mindlessly. This warning applies with greater force to the larger and more rampant *C. poscharskyana*.

C. pulla, 3in (7.5cm), is a plant with a running habit that forms loose mats and in summer produces nodding violet-blue flowers.

Cultivation: The campanulas described are plants for free-draining soil and positions in full sun or light shade. Most species are easily raised from seed and can be propagated from cuttings taken in late spring or early summer or by division.

Cassiope

The cassiopes are small evergreen shrubby members of the heather family that demand acid conditions and a moist soil. They are attractive plants for the peat bed and can be pot-grown effectively in the alpine house.

C. lycopodioides, 3in (7.5cm), is a mat-forming plant, spreading as much as 18in (45cm). The wiry stems are densely covered with tiny leaves; the dainty bell-like flowers are borne in late spring.

C. mertensiana 'Gracilis', 2in (5cm), makes a spreading mound, some 12in (30cm) across, of pale green leaves. In late spring and early summer it bears white flowers.

C. tetragona, 12–18in (30–45cm), is a plant of dark green leaves and erect growth that in late spring produces hanging white flowers, commonly tinged pink.

Cultivation: Plant in a cool position in light shade where the soil is lime-free. Propagate from cuttings or by layering.

Celmisia

These evergreen mountain daisies native to Australia and New Zealand are not all as difficult as their reputation might suggest. They are worth a place in the scree garden, for instance, not only for their flowers but also for their foliage, which in many species is strikingly silvered or white felted.

C. argentea, 3in (7.5cm), is a miniature species good for a sink garden. The woolly stemless flowers appear in early summer.

C. bellidioides, 1in (2.5cm), a low-

Campanula

The bellflowers, as they are popularly known, include some of the loveliest and most useful rock garden plants. Some of the truly alpine species are a great test of the enthusiast's skill but others are dependable rock garden plants that give a profuse display of flowers in summer.

C. arvatica, 3in (7.5cm) does best in a scree bed or planted in a crevice. The starry violet flowers are borne in mid-summer over a mat of mid-green leaves. There is also a white form, 'Alba'.

C. aucheri, 2in (5cm), makes a miniature tuft of toothed leaves. The relatively large purplish-blue flowers appear in the early summer months.

C. carpatica, 4–8in (10–20cm), is a vigorous tufted plant with trailing stems and is an excellent plant for the large rock garden. The large open bell flowers, blue or white, are borne for a long period from mid-summer. 'Ditton Blue' has deep blue flowers and 'Turbinata' is a compact blue-flowered form with grayish leaves.

C. cochlearifolia (syn. *C. pusilla*), 3in (7.5cm), is an easy plant that spreads by underground runners. The hanging flowers are borne on wiry stems over compact mats

growing species making close mats of dark green leaves above which the white flowers with bright orange centers appear in the early months of summer.

C. coriacea, 12in (30cm), forms clumps of pointed silvery leaves and produces large daisy flowers in summer borne on stout stems.

Cultivation: Celmisias need lime-free soil that although well-drained has a plentiful supply of water. They do best in lightly shaded positions. In winter those with felted leaves may need overhead protection from excessive wet. Seed germination is often not straightforward. Cuttings and division are the easiest methods of propagation.

Chamaecyparis *see* Conifers.

Chionodoxa

The common name glory-of-the-snow indicates the alpine origin of this small group of spring-flowering bulbs.

C. gigantea, 18in (20cm), the largest-flowered species and possibly merely a large form of *C. luciliae*, produces, from late winter to mid-spring, lax flower-spikes with up to three white-centered violet-blue flowers.

C. luciliae, 6in (15cm), is the most commonly grown species. In early spring the loose flower-spikes carry up to 10 bright blue flowers with white centers. Pink forms are also available.

C. sardensis, 6in (15cm), is similar to *C. luciliae* but the flowers are a deeper blue.

Cultivation: Despite their alpine origins, chionodoxas are not difficult to grow. In autumn plant in any well-drained soil in full sun. Little further attention is required. If plants become overcrowded, lift and divide as leaves die down after flowering. Seed sets freely.

Conifers

The dwarf conifers are among the most useful evergreen plants for giving the rock garden or raised bed year-round interest. In the vast range available they show great variation in habit, texture and coloring. New cultivars are constantly being introduced into commerce; the plants listed below are only a small selection of the best-known varieties.

Abies balsamea 'Hudsonia', 3ft (1m), has dark green foliage with bluish white bands on the reverse. In spring the new growth on these round-topped dwarf firs contrasts attractively with the old foliage.

Chamaecyparis lawsoniana 'Minima Aurea', 5ft (1.5m), is a dwarf false cypress of very slow growth. The twisted foliage is bright yellow.

C. obtusa 'Nana', 24in (60cm), is a very slow-growing flat-topped plant with dark green leaves.

Cryptomeria japonica 'Compressa', 3ft (1m), is a dwarf form of the Japanese cedar that makes a rounded plant with congested foliage that takes on bronze coloring in the winter months.

Juniperus communis 'Compressa', 1m (3ft), is one of the most widely planted dwarf conifers. It makes a dense column of blue-green foliage that is very slow growing.

J. squamata 'Blue Star', 3ft (1m), is a relatively new introduction of exceptional merit. The mound of silver-blue foliage is particularly bright throughout the summer.

Picea abies 'Little Gem', 24in (60cm), makes a dense, cushion-shaped bush of tiny leaves, with bright new shoots in spring.

P. mariana 'Nana', 12in (30cm), is one of the smallest of the dwarf conifers, suitable even for a sink garden. It makes a compact bun of soft blue-green leaves.

Pinus sylvestris 'Beuvronensis', 5ft (1.5m), is a blue-grey dwarf form of the Scots pine. The dense branching of the young plant generally opens out with age.

Thuja occidentalis 'Danica', 3ft (1m), a dwarf American white cedar, makes a

Opposite *(top) The campanulas, or bellflowers, include annuals, biennials and perennials for all types of rock garden.*
(below) Chionodoxa luciliae *is an attractive spring-flowering bulb.*

Above *Dwarf conifers are available in a remarkable range of colors, shapes and textures and add some height and interest to a rock garden.*

Above *The brightly-coloured brooms do best in an open, sunny position.*

Above right *Crocus chrysanthus 'Blue Pearl' is an excellent named form of this popular plant.*

compact rounded bush with foliage that remains bright green throughout the year.

T. orientalis 'Aurea Nana', 5ft (1.5m), is a striking golden yellow dwarf conifer that makes a dense rounded bush of vertical sprays.

Tsuga canadensis 'Bennetts Dwarf' 3ft (1m), is a dwarf hemlock with graceful arching branches of mid-green foliage.

Cultivation: Grow dwarf conifers in reasonably moisture-retentive soil in full sun or partial shade (those with golden foliage will lose this coloring if planted in shade). At planting time ensure that trees are firmed in and well watered. Plants will benefit from an annual feed of a slow-release fertilizer.

Corydalis

The dwarf perennials of this genus are attractive for their finely divided foliage and for their quaint tubular flowers.

C. cashmeriana, 6in (15cm), a bulbous species, has bright green leaves and flowers of brilliant blue tinged green that appear in spring and early summer.

C. cheilanthifolia, 8in (20cm), is a yellow-flowered species that has pretty fern-like leaves with a slightly bronzed tinge. It flowers over a long season starting in the late spring.

Cultivation: C. cashmeriana is a rather demanding and generally short-lived plant that requires lime-free soil and a moist atmosphere. Plant the tubers in autumn. The other species are easily satisfied and are more likely to need thinning than special cultivation.

Crocus

These deservedly popular bulbous plants are among the best dwarf subjects for bringing color into the rock garden in late winter and early spring. There are also useful and lovely species that flower in autumn. The large Dutch crocuses are more at home in the border or naturalized in grass than in the rock garden so they have not been included in this selection of species and their wonderfully varied forms.

C. chrysanthus, 3in (7.5cm), is best known for the wide range of forms of which it is a parent. Most of those mentioned flower in early spring or even late winter: 'Advance', pale yellow and bronze; 'Blue Bird', blue and cream; 'Blue Pearl', pale blue and white; 'Goldilocks', deep yellow and purple base; 'Ladykiller', purple with white interior; 'Snow Bunting', white marked with purple and having an orange base; 'Zwanenburg Bronze', bronze outside and deep yellow inside.

C. imperati, 4in (10cm), flowers in late winter. The inner petals are purple, the

outer biscuit color streaked with purple.

C. minimus, 2in (5cm), has dull yellow flowers variously veined and feathered with deep purple, which open in the early and mid-spring.

C. speciosus, 5in (12.5cm), is an autumn-flowering species and one of the easiest to grow. The lilac-blue flowers are finely veined in dark purple. Named forms include: 'Oxonian', dark blue flowers; 'Aitchisonii', large with pale mauve flowers; and 'Albus', white.

C. tomasinianus, 3in (7.5cm), is an easy species that flowers in late winter and early spring. There is considerable variation in color from pale mauve to deep purple. Two dark-flowered forms, 'Barr's Purple' and 'Whitewell Purple', are particularly attractive to look at.

Cultivation: In rock gardens or raised beds plant groups of corms as soon as they become available in well-drained soil in full sun. Crocuses are excellent as pan-grown plants in the alpine house. The easiest method of propagation is from the small cormlets produced by the parent corms. Plants can be raised from seed but cross-pollination may mean that seed will not come true.

Cryptomeria *see* Conifers.

Cyclamen

The hardy dwarf cyclamen are plants of strong family resemblance. They grow from corms, producing leaves that are often handsomely mottled and all have elegant flowers in white, pink or carmine with reflexed petals. There are few plants of greater quality for the rock garden and if several species are grown they provide almost year-round interest.

C. coum (syn. C. orbiculatum), 3in (7.5cm), makes a close little plant of rounded leaves, red underneath and sometimes prettily mottled. The flowers, about ¾in (18mm) long are borne from late winter till early spring.

C. hederifolium (syn. C. neapolitanum), 4in (10cm), is an autumn-flowering species with leaves that are frequently patterned with silvery markings. They persist into late spring, making a useful contribution themselves to the beauty of the rock garden. The flowers, which are borne over a long season, are about 1in (2.5cm) long.

C. purpurascems (syn. C. europaeum), 4in (10cm), has mid-green kidney-shaped leaves with light silvery patterning. The fragrant flowers are generally carmine.

Cultivation: Plant corms in late summer in well-drained soil which has had peat or leaf mold added to it. Choose sheltered positions in light shade. Corms take time to settle down – and resent disturbance. Cyclamen set seed freely (the corms do not produce offsets) and plants can be brought to flowering size in about three to four years.

Cytisus
This genus of brooms includes several free-flowering small shrubs that provide a strong splash of color in late spring or early summer.

C. ardoinii, 6in (15cm), is a deciduous mat-forming species with downy leaves that has a spread of about 1ft (30cm). The flowers are bright yellow.

C. × beanii, 24in (60cm), a deciduous shrub with yellow flowers that forms a spreading bush up to 3ft (1m) wide.

C. × kewensis, 24in (60cm), deciduous, is a plant for the large rock garden as it can spread up to 4ft (1.2m). However, its profuse display of creamy yellow flowers makes it a worthwhile plant for those who have the room.

Cultivation: Brooms do well in almost any soil provided they have a sunny position and well-drained soil. Species can be grown from seed and propagated from cuttings. As plants transplant badly, start seeds and cuttings in single pots and when ready plant out directly in their final positions.

Daphne
The daphnes, evergreen and deciduous shrubs, include a number of dwarf species suitable for the rock garden. The individual flowers, generally sweetly scented, are quite small but they are borne in profusion.

D. arbuscula, 6in (15cm), evergreen, makes a tidy bush of dark green lustrous

Above Dianthus *'La Bourboulle'*, a low growing plant for the rock garden: the flowers grow on very short stems.

leaves. In mid-summer there are clusters of rosy scented flowers.

D. cneorum, 6in (15cm), the garland flower, makes an evergreen twiggy plant that bears masses of scented pink flowers in early summer. D. c. 'Alba' has white flowers and D. c. 'Eximia' is a particularly good form with flowers that are larger and deeper pink than the type.

Cultivation: Although not always long-lived, daphnes are not fussy about soil provided it is well drained. Plant in sun or partial shade, preferably where the roots are shaded by a large rock or by other plants. Daphnes transplant badly so stock raised from seed or cuttings should be grown in individual pots and planted out young in the permanent position. Layering is a slow but useful method of propagation.

Dianthus
This large genus includes not only dwarf dianthus – which are excellent plants for the rock garden, the scree bed and in a paving – but also the florist's pinks and carnations. Among the large number of perennial species that are natives of rocky and alpine environments the family resemblance is very strong. The five-petaled flowers are generally borne in early summer above tufty clumps of narrow leaves.

Above Dryas octopetala, *the mountain avens, a trailing, mat-forming evergreen for the rock garden.*

Below right and opposite *The Epidmediums are hardy perennials grown for their decorative foliage and delicate flowers.*

D. alpinus, 3in (7.5cm), has large flowers in relation to the size of the clump, which is of deep green leaves. There is considerable variation in the shading of the flowers, which are not fragrant, but they are generally rose-purple with a central pale eye surrounded by a ring of dark spots.

D. deltoides, 10in (25cm), the maiden pink, is a mat-forming plant with narrow rich green leaves. The small deep pink flowers are borne over a long period in summer. Named forms include the bright pink 'Brilliant' and the striking crimson 'Flashing Light'.

D. gratianopolitanus (syn. *D. caesius*), 8in (20cm), commonly known in U.S. as the Cheddar pink, forms mats of grayish leaves as much as 24in (60cm) across. The single pink flowers are fragrant. *D. g.* 'Flore Pleno' is a double form of compact growth.

D. neglectus, 4–8in (10–20cm), makes a tufty growth of mid-green leaves and bears flowers that can vary in color from light pink to dark crimson but characteristically the underside of the petal is buff.

In addition to the species listed there are a number of dwarf hybrids, generally growing no more than 6in (15cm), that are not out of place in the rock garden. These include: 'Dubarry', deep pink; 'Fanal', bright pink; 'Fusilier', crimson; 'La Bourboulle', pink and also available in a white form; 'Little Jock', rose pink with darker eye; 'Mars', red; 'Pike's Pink', pink; and 'White Bouquet', white.

Cultivation: Many dianthus thrive in sharply drained limy soil in full sun. Most will do well in a sandy loam. Note, however, that *D. neglectus* dislikes lime and that *D. alpinus* is fairly tolerant of acid soils and does best with some light shade. Some of those described are not long-lived; it is worth taking cuttings in summer to ensure that vigorous stock is maintained. Plants of true species can be grown from seed sown in spring or early summer.

Draba

This large genus includes a number of perennial species native to harsh and mountainous regions that are well-suited to rock gardens, scree beds or, in the case of the more difficult, cultivation in the alpine house. They are characteristically cushion-forming plants with cross-shaped yellow flowers.

D. aizoides, 4in (10cm), forms a mat of inconspicuously bristled grayish leaves that can spread up to 10in (25cm) across. The pale yellow flowers, which are about ¼in (6mm) across, are borne in mid-spring.

D. bryoides (syn. *D. rigida bryoides*), 1in (2.5cm), forms a dense cushion up to 3in (7.5cm) wide. The yellow flowers are borne in early and mid-spring.

D. mollissima, 1in (2.5cm), makes downy hummocks of tightly packed rosettes, which in late spring and early summer are covered with bright yellow flowers.

D. rigida, 4in (10cm), consists of tiny rosettes of mid-green leaves over which the deep yellow flowers are borne profusely in mid-spring.

Cultivation: All the drabas listed require sharp drainage, although in spring and until

flowering they need a plentiful supply of moisture. In the rock garden they are often best accommodated in a crevice. Those with downy leaves, such as *D. mollissima*, need protection from the wet in winter and are therefore often pot-grown in an alpine house. Plants can be propagated from seed sown in spring or from cuttings consisting of non-flowering rosettes taken in summer.

Dryas

One of the two species of this genus, an evergreen prostrate shrub native to the mountains of Europe, is a lovely rock garden plant.

D. octopetala, 4in (10cm), makes a spreading mat of glossy oak-like leaves, downy on the underside, some 24in (60cm) across. The broad eight-petalled flowers, white with an orange center, are borne, sometimes rather sparsely, in the early to mid-summer months and followed by feathery seed heads.
Cultivation: Grow in ordinary well-drained soil in a sunny position. Plants dislike disturbance. Propagate from seed sown when ripe or from selected cuttings taken in late summer.

Epimedium

The dwarf epimediums are useful plants for shady parts of the rock garden. It is mainly for their leaves that they are grown, but their flowers have a beauty of their own.

E. alpinum, 10in (25cm), a deciduous species, has toothed leaves divided into two or three heart-shaped leaflets. In spring there are several dark red flowers marked with yellow.

E. grandiflorum (syn. *E. macranthum*), 10in (25cm), a deciduous clump-forming plant with toothed triangular leaflets. Flowers, varying in color from violet to white, are borne in early summer. The selected form 'Rose Queen' is a deep pink color in flower.

E. × rubrum, 12in (30cm), has foliage that is handsomely tinted bronze-red when young. The flowers, which appear in late spring, are crimson.

Erica

Provided that they are planted in moderation, the dwarf forms of heather make a useful contribution to the rock garden by virtue of their attractive evergreen foliage and their winter flowering season.

E. carnea (syn. *E. herbacea*), 6–8in (15–21cm), is a very variable species with numerous dwarf named forms. The following is merely an introduction to the range available: 'Eileen Porter', deep red; 'Springwood Pink' and 'Springwood White', pink and white forms that flower particularly densely; 'Vivelii', crimson flowers and dark foliage.
Cultivation: Unlike many heathers, *E. carnea* is lime-tolerant. Grow plants in freely-draining soil in full sun. To keep growth vigorous and close shear off spent flower heads when they have faded. Propagate from cuttings with a heel, taken in late summer, or by layering.

Erinus

The single evergreen species that makes up this genus is a suitable plant for the rock or sink garden and is an attractive colonizer of wall and paving crevices.

E. alpinus, 3in (7.5cm), forms tufty mounds of toothed hairy leaves. The tubular flowers, which are borne in a long season throughout spring and summer, are rosy-purple. Named varieties include: 'Albus', white; 'Dr Hanele', carmine and the larger 'Mrs Charles Boyle', pink.
Cultivation: Grow in full sun or light shade in any sharply drained soil. Plants are generally not long-lived but are easily raised from seed.

Erodium

The scientific name derived from the Greek for 'heron' and the common name stork's bill are allusions to the beaked form of the fruit. These close relatives of the geraniums include a number of perennial and sub-shrubby plants of compact growth.

E. chrysanthum, 6in (15cm), has pretty finely cut silvery leaves and yellow flowers that are borne throughout summer.

E. corsicum, 8in (20cm), forms spreading

Above Erinus alpinus *is a tufted, hardy plant which is very suitable for most types of rock garden.*

Above Erodium corsicum, *a summer-flowering, mat-forming perennial.*

Below Erythronium tuolumnense, *a hardy bulbous plant, 9–12 inches (23–30 centimeters) in height, that flowers in March and April.*

tufts of downy gray-green leaves about 10in (25cm) wide. The flowers, pale pink veined red, are borne from mid-spring to early summer.

E. reichardii (syn. *E. chamaedryoides*), 2in (5cm), is like a more compact version of *E. corsicum.* The flowers are white with purple veining. There is a pink form, 'Roseum'.

Cultivation: Erodiums need full sun and prefer a well-drained limy soil. *E. corsicum* and *E. reichardii* should be given sheltered positions and *E. corsicum*, in particular, should be given protection from excessive wet in winter. Plants can be propagated from seed, by division, or from cuttings of roots or basal shoots that are hardy.

Erythronium

The lily-like erythroniums are spring-flowering bulbs of great beauty for a cool and lightly shaded spot in the rock garden. These all have nodding flowers with reflexed petals.

E. dens-canis, 9in (23cm), the dog's-tooth violet, has mid-green foliage with darker mottling and rose-pink flowers. Named forms include: 'Pink Perfection', clear pink; 'Rose Beauty', deep pink; and 'White Splendour', white.

E. revolutum, 12in (30cm), the trout lily, has mottled foliage and flowers in shades from pink to purple with deeper markings.

E. tuolumnense, 10in (25cm), has bright green leaves and yellow flowers. Hybrids of which this plant is a parent include: 'Kondo' and 'Pagoda', both yellow.

Cultivation: Erythroniums require a moist and reasonably rich soil. Plant the corms deeply when available. They resent disturbances. Propagate from seed or from offsets.

Festuca

Among this genus of grasses are some relatively dwarf evergreen species that are useful in the rock garden for the contrast created by their linear foliage.

F. alpina, 4in (10cm), forms clumps of fine bright green leaves. In late summer there are green flowers tinged purple.

F. glauca, 10in (25cm), is a lovely blue-grey plant that looks attractive among paving as well as in the rock garden. It bears purple flowers in mid-summer.

Cultivation: Grow these plants in ordinary well-drained soil in full sun. When flower heads have faded remove them to avoid plants shedding seeds. Plants can be raised easily from seed or by division.

Gaultheria

Among this genus are hardy evergreen shrubs that are useful plants for lightly shaded, lime-free areas of the rock garden. The urn-like or bell-shaped flowers are followed by attractive berries.

G. cuneata, 12in (30cm), is a compact shrub with dark green leaves. The white flowers are borne in summer and followed by a striking display of rounded white berries.

G. miqueliana, 12in (30cm), may spread as much as 3ft (1m). The clusters of small white flowers, borne in early summer, are followed by white fruit that often show a pink tinge.

G. procumbens, 6in (15cm), an American species, is a creeping carpet-forming plant. In late summer there are white or pinkish flowers and in autumn red berries.

Cultivation: Plant in moisture-retentive acid soil. These dwarf species are well suited to peat beds in partial shade. Propagate from seed or from cuttings with a heel taken in summer.

Genista

Among these members of the broom family are several low-growing deciduous shrubs that in early summer give a handsome display of yellow flowers.

G. pilosa, 18in (45cm), is an almost evergreen shrub that may spread as much as 4ft (1.2m). The prostrate form, *G. p.* 'Procumbens', is ground-hugging and rarely exceeds 3in (7.5cm). In early summer the plants are covered in a mass of small yellow flowers.

G. sagittalis, 6in (15cm), is a mat-forming

plant that is rather sparsely leafed although the winged stems have a rather leaf-life appearance. The flowers are borne, in the early to mid-summer months, on very erect stems.

Cultivation: Grow in sunny positions where the soil is well-drained but moisture-retentive. Propagate straight from seed or from selected basal cuttings taken in the spring months.

Gentiana

The gentians are a large group of herbaceous plants that include some of the loveliest of all alpine perennials. The flowers are generally funnel-like or bell-shaped, and in the best known species are sumptuous blues.

G. acaulis, 3in (7.5cm), is a spring-flowering European species. It is not a difficult plant to grow in an open position with loamy soil, and its deep blue stemless flowers spotted green in the throat are of ravishing beauty. However, flowering can be erratic.

G. farreri, 4in (10cm), an Asiatic species with prostrate stems some 12in (30cm) long. The solitary flowers, borne in late summer at the end of stems, are Cambridge blue with greenish spotting and banding, and shade to white in the throat.

G. × macaulayi, 6in (15cm), is an autumn-flowering hybrid of Asiatic species. In growth it is similar to *G. farreri* but the flowers are deep blue.

G. septemfida, 6in (15cm), is an Asiatic species and one of the easiest gentians to grow. The flowers are borne in clusters in summer. The flower color is variable but good forms are deep blue with lighter markings in the throat.

G. sino-ornata, 4in (10cm), another Asiatic species of prostrate growth with stems up to 12in (30cm) long. The flowers, which are borne singly in the autumn, are rich blue striped deep purple and green in color.

G. verna, 3in (7.5cm), the spring gentian, is a native of the European Alps. This rosette-forming plant produces starry flowers of brilliant blue. *G. v.* 'Angulosa' is a robust form.

Cultivation: In general the Asiatic species, which flower in summer and autumn, are the easiest to grow, although they demand lime-free soil. The European and Asiatic species require a sunny position (*G. × macaulayi* will tolerate light shade) and free drainage. Some species, including *G. acaulis* and *G. sino-ornata,* can be propagated by division in spring but others resent disturbance. Seed can be sown in early spring but it can take up to a year to germinate.

Geranium

The common name, crane's-bill, and the scientific name are an allusion to the beaked fruit of these plants. The crane's-bills include a number of dwarf species that are excellent rock garden plants that are attractive in leaf and flower.

G. cinereum, 6in (15cm), has prettily lobed downy leaves and in spring produces pink flowers with darker veining. *G. c.* 'Ballerina' has flowers that are almost white richly veined crimson-purple.

G. dalmaticum, 4in (10cm), is a clump-forming species with glossy five-lobed leaves. These often turn red in autumn. In summer there are numerous pink flowers.

Above *The pink-flowered* Geranium dalmaticum.

Below *Between them the many different types of gentian can provide glorious blue flowers throughout the spring and summer.*

Top Hebe *'Carl Teschner'*, a dense spreading plant with violet flowers.

Above Hebe pinguifolia *'Pagei'* is a good form of the white flowered bush.

Above right *Helianthemums*, or rock roses, are very free flowering perennials.

G. farreri (syn. *G. napuligerum*), 6in (15cm), forms a slow-growing mat of deeply lobed leaves. The flowers, which are pink with black anthers, are borne over a long season starting in late spring.

G. sanguineum 'Lancastriense', 3in (7.5cm), makes a spreading plant some 1ft (30cm) across. There is a long display of pink flowers throughout the summer.

G. subcaulescens, 6in (15cm), is similar to *G. cinereum* but the flowers are not veined.
Cultivation: Grow in ordinary well-drained soil in full sun. Propagate from seed sown in spring or by division.

Gypsophila

The cushion-forming habit of several dwarf alpine species is in sharp contrast to the frothy growth of the common gypsophila of borders *(G. paniculata)*.

G. aetioides, 2in (5cm), makes a miniature hard gray-green cushion that is dotted with white or pale pink flowers in early summer.

G. cerastioides, 3in (7.5cm), forms spreading clumps of gray-green leaves up to 1½ft (45cm) wide. There is a long succession of white flowers with purple veins from summer to autumn.

G. repens (syn. *G. dubia*), 6in (15cm), is the most commonly grown alpine species. It makes a wide-spreading plant, to 2ft (60cm) across, with wiry stems and gray-green leaves. The small white to pink flowers are borne profusely throughout the summer months.

Cultivation: Grow in full sun in any well-drained soil. *G. repens* should be planted so that the stems can cascade down rocks or a wall. *G. aetioides* is probably best pot-grown in an alpine house. Plants can be propagated from seed, by division, and from cuttings.

Hebe

The hebes or shrubby evergreen veronicas are for the most part from New Zealand so it is not surprising that some have not proved fully hardy in the East. However, there are several dwarf species that are attractive shrubs for the rock garden and these are reasonably hardy.

H. buchananii 'Minor', 4in (10cm), is a really miniature little shrub with wiry stems and rounded leaves. The white flowers appear in early summer.

H. 'Carl Teschner', 12in (30cm), is a hybrid of dense habit with a spread up to 24in (60cm). The leaves are gray-green and the violet flowers are carried throughout the summer.

H. 'Pagei' (syn. *H. pinguifolia* 'Pagei'), 10in (25cm), can make a spreading bush up to 30in (75cm) broad. The blue-green leaves with a reddish margin are an attractive feature. The white flowers are borne in early summer.
Cultivation: Grow in any well-drained soil in full sun. *H. buchananii* 'Minor' makes a good subject for a sink garden. Hebe cuttings strike readily. Plants can also be

Left *Helianthemum, the rock rose, a very free flowering perennial plant.*

Below Hypericum fragile *is deep yellow in color.*

grown from seed but as hebes hybridize freely plants may not come true.

Helianthemum

The helianthemums or rock roses are free-flowering easy evergreen shrubs for creating a broad effect in the rock garden. However, they should not be associated with quieter, less vigorous, species.

H. lunulatum, 6in (15cm), makes a neat clump of gray foliage and bears yellow flowers in summer.

H. nummularium (syn. *H. chamaecistus*), 12in (30cm), is a mat-forming European species with golden-yellow flowers in summer. From it are derived many cultivated gray-leaved forms that flower prolifically in the summer. These include: 'Ben Heckla', deep bronze; 'Ben Hope', red with orange center; 'Mrs C. W. Earle', double scarlet; 'Sterntaler', yellow; 'The Bride', white; 'Wisley Pink', warm pink; and 'Wisley Primrose', yellow.

Cultivation: Grow in ordinary well-drained soil in full sun. Plants of named forms should be propagated from heeled cuttings in summer.

Hypericum

The common name, St John's wort, refers to the traditional belief that the plant was a protection against the devil. A less fanciful reason for growing the dwarf shrubby species is that they give a fine display of golden flowers in summer.

H. coris, 6in (15cm), is a neat little shrublet with yellow flowers borne in mid-summer.

H. fragile, 10in (25cm), a woody-based perennial, has gray-green foliage and bears yellow flowers with a slight red tinge in the late summer months.

H. olympicum, 10in (25cm), with which *H. fragile* has often been confused, makes a spreading shrub up to 1ft (30cm) wide with gray-green leaves. The bright yellow flowers are borne at the tips of stems in mid- to late summer. *H. o.* 'Citrinum' is a form with pale yellow flowers.

H. polyphyllum, 8in (20cm), is very close to *H. olympicum* except for minor botanical distinctions. The form 'Sulphureum' has pale yellow flowers.

H. reptans, 3in (7.5cm), is a deciduous species making small mats of mid-green leaves and producing a late-summer display of yellow flowers that are reddish in bud.

Cultivation: Plant in ordinary well-drained soil in sunny positions. Propagate from soft basal cuttings taken in early summer.

Iberis

Among the candytufts, probably best known for the annual species, are several perennials that are useful in the rock garden.

I. saxatilis, 4in (10cm), is a prostrate evergreen shrub that is a true alpine. The small white flowers are borne in the early summer months.

I. sempervirens, 6in (15cm), makes a

spreading bushy plant that gives a striking display of massed white flowers in late spring and early summer. 'Snowflake' is a more spreading plant with larger flowers; 'Little Gem' is a neater more erect form than the type.

Cultivation: Plant in any well-drained soil in a sunny position. *I. saxatilis* is a suitable plant for a scree bed. Propagate from softwood cuttings taken in summer.

Iris

The dwarf irises rank among the best bulbs for planting in the rock garden or for growing in pots in the alpine house. They are easy plants to grow, flower early, when the garden is still rather bare, and yet, despite their delicate appearance, withstand cold, rough weather remarkably well. They are commonly called reticulata irises, a reference to the net-like sheath around the bulb.

I. danfordiae, 4in (10cm), produces greenish-yellow flowers in late winter.

I. histrioides 'Major', 4in (10cm), flowers before the leaves appear in late winter. The flower color, a vibrant deep blue, is set off by the bright orange crest.

I. reticulata, 6in (15cm), which flowers in late winter and early spring, has leaves first developing as the flowers come out. The

Above *The combination of different rock plants, such as iberis, saxifrage and dwarf rhododendrons will make a colorful rock garden.*

Right *The lewisias are delicate little plants with star-shaped petals, most commonly available in shades of pink, rose and salmon.*

common form has violet-blue flowers. Named forms include: 'Cantab', light blue; 'J. S. Dijt', reddish-purple; 'Clairette', bright blue and white; and 'Royal Blue', deep blue.

Cultivation: Plant the bulbs in small clumps in well-drained sunny positions, preferably in slightly limy soil. Most of these irises will establish themselves and maintain colonies. *I. danfordiae,* however, has a tendency to split up into numerous tiny bulblets that take a number of years to reach flowering size. The bulbous irises are most easily propagated from offsets.

Juniperus *see* Conifers.

Leontopodium

The edelweiss, a native of the European Alps, is an interesting plant that is worth a place in the rock garden.

L. alpinum, 6in (15cm), is a grayish woolly plant that in spring produces starry bracts which surround asymmetrical heads of ray-less flowers.

Cultivation: Grow in well-drained soil in sunny positions. Propagate from seed.

Leucojum

The leucojums or snowflakes, can be distinguished from snowdrops by the fact that the petals on the nodding flowers of the former are all of the same size.

L. autumnale, 10in (25cm), flowers in autumn before the leaves develop or just as they emerge. The flowers are white tinged pink at the base.

L. vernum, 8in (20cm), the spring snowflake, has strap-like green leaves and white flowers.

Cultivation: Plant in well-drained soil, *L. autumnale* in full sun, *L. vernum* in sun or light shade. Propagate from seed or offsets.

Lewisia

The lewisias are rather succulent rosette-forming perennials which are attractive in the rock garden or alpine house for their showy flowers in spring and early summer.

L. cotyledon, 12in (30cm), forms tufts of fleshy leaves that sometimes have a wavy edge. The flowers range in color from white to coral. This species has given rise to many attractive forms and hybrids, such as: 'George Henley', brick red; 'Pinkie', pink; and 'Rose Splendor', warm pink. Some forms, such as *L. c.* 'Heckneri' (large-flowered and bright pink) and *L. c. howellii* (pink with deeper markings) have sometimes been treated as separate species.

L. tweedyi, 6in (15cm), is an evergreen species that produces a single flower per stem. The color can vary from a lovely, soft pale pink to apricot.

Cultivation: Grow in sharply draining neutral soil in an open position. Lewisias are prone to rotting in wet weather so surround the neck of plants with a layer of chips. Another way to avoid rotting is to plant lewisias in the crevices of walls. In the alpine house water sparingly after flowering. Plants can be grown from offsets taken in summer. Lewisias hybridize freely but seed, although it may not come true, is an easy means of propagation.

Linum

Several of the perennial and sub-shrubby flaxes make good rock garden plants that are useful for their sustained displays of bright flowers.

L. flavum, 15in (45cm), forms mounds of gray-green foliage and bears a profuse display of yellow flowers in the summer.

L. narbonense, 18in (45cm), is a rather tall species that is useful in a large rock garden for its long season of blue flowers.

L. perenne alpinum, 12in (30cm), is an alpine form of the perennial flax. The sky-blue flowers are borne over a long period in summer.

Cultivation: The flaxes are easy plants given full sun and well-drained soil. They are not long-lived but are easily grown from seed or propagated from cuttings taken in spring.

Top Leontopodium alpinum *is the well-known edelweiss, a popular plant for the rock garden.*

Above *The leucojums are hardy, bulbous plants with flowers that resemble large snowdrops.*

Right *The Oxford and Cambridge muscari,* M. tubergenianum, *has flowers of pale and dark blue in March and April.*

Below Lithospermum oleifolium, *not often grown, is an attractive rock garden plant, with deep blue flowers.*

Lithospermum

The lithospermums include a number of hardy ground-hugging plants that produce bright blue funnel-shaped flowers. Although botanists have now placed those listed here under *Lithodora*, in commerce they generally go under their old name.

L. diffusum, 4in (10cm), makes a spreading plant up to 24in (60cm) wide that flowers in summer. Two widely grown forms, 'Grace Ward' and 'Heavenly Blue', have flowers that are larger than the type and of a more intense blue.

L. oleifolium, 6in (15cm), is a smaller plant than *L. diffusum* and in bud the flowers show a pink tinge.

Cultivation: L. diffusum and its forms must have lime-free soil but otherwise these are not difficult plants given a sunny position and well-drained soil. Propagate from cuttings taken in summer.

Muscari

The common grape hyacinth, *M. neglectum,* spreads too vigorously from small offsets to make it an ideal plant for the rock garden. However, there are other choice spring-flowering species with the characteristic flowering spikes of crowded bells.

M. armeniacum, 8in (20cm), produces in mid-spring flower spikes of scented deep-blue bells with a white margin. 'Cantab' has pale clear blue flowers and 'Heavenly Blue' is a fine bright blue.

M. botryoides, 8in (20cm), is one of the best for the rock garden. Flowering early to mid-spring, it produces china-blue bells with white at the mouth. The white form,

'Album', is particularly good.

M. tubergenianum (syn. *M. aucheri*), 8in (20cm), is an early-spring species with an attractive contrast between the pale blue of the upper sterile flowers and the deep blue of the lower flowers. It is sometimes listed as 'Oxford and Cambridge'.

Cultivation: Plant in full sun in ordinary well-drained soil. The more vigorous species will need to be lifted and divided every three years. Plants raised from seed can be brought to flower in about three years. Most species produce offsets freely and these provide an easy method of propagation.

Narcissus

Among the spring-flowering bulbs the daffodils and jonquils have long been considered plants of the first importance. In addition to the large-growing narcissi that are used for planting in borders and in grass, there are numerous true species and cultivated forms of dwarf habit. These are ideal for the rock garden or raised bed and are lovely when grown as pot-grown plants in the alpine house.

N. 'Baby Moon', 20cm (8in), a dwarf hybrid jonquil, has numerous fragrant yellow flowers to a stem.

N. 'Beryl', 8in (20cm), is a hybrid derived from *N. cyclamineus* that has an orange cup and yellow swept-back petals.

N. bulbocodium, 2–6in (5–15cm), is commonly known as the hoop petticoat daffodil on account of the distinctive funnel-shaped trumpet or corona, which is generally crinkled at the margin. This species, which flowers in late winter and early spring, is very variable in color as well as size, ranging from white to deep yellow. The naming of the numerous forms is somewhat confusing but all are plants of great beauty. *N. b. romieuxii* is a lovely pale yellow form that is best suited to pot culture in the alpine house.

N. cantabricus, 4in (10cm), is very close to *N. bulbocodium* but has more open, white coronas.

N. cyclamineus, 8in (20cm), has hanging golden flowers with narrow trumpets and reflexed petals. It begins flowering in the early spring.

N. 'February Gold', 10in (25cm), is not one of the real miniatures but is a sturdy and useful deep yellow trumpet hybrid that flowers in late winter and early spring.

N. 'February Silver', 10in (25cm), is similar to the foregoing except that the petals are creamy white.

N. 'Jack Snipe', 8in (20cm), another hybrid derived from *N. cyclamineus*, has cream petals and a yellow trumpet.

N. juncifolius, 6in (15cm), is a miniature jonquil with up to five deep yellow flowers to a stem.

N. minor, 8in (20cm), a dwarf trumpet-daffodil in which the petals are paler yellow than the trumpet.

N. 'Tête-à-Tête', 8in (20cm), is a very early-flowering hybrid that produces two or more yellow trumpets to a stem.

N. triandrus albus, to 10in (25cm), popularly known as the angel's tears daffodil, bears two or three pendent creamy-yellow flowers to a stem in early spring.

Cultivation: Plant bulbs as soon as they become available in autumn. Group them in irregular clumps in any ordinary well-drained sunny or lightly shaded position. The most vigorous miniatures can be planted to grow through creeping perennial rock garden plants. Most will naturalize readily. Clumps can be lifted and divided when the leaves die down if they become congested. Offsets provide the easiest method of propagation.

Oenothera

The evening primroses are showy plants with large funnel-shaped flowers, which, as the common name suggests, open up in the evening.

O. acaulis, 6in (15cm), makes a dandelion-like clump of leaves. The stemless flowers, white fading to pink, are borne over a long season in the summer.

O. missouriensis, 6in (15cm), is a lax plant with a spread of 18in (45cm). The large yellow flowers, produced over a long season in summer, are flushed red in the bud.

O. perennis (syn. *O. pumila*), 12in (30cm),

is a less showy plant than the others, bearing small yellow flowers in mid-summer.
Cultivation: These are easy plants for ordinary well-drained soil and sunny positions. *O. acaulis* is often treated as a biennial. Grow plants from seed or propagate by division or from cuttings.

Papaver

Although generally short-lived, the dwarf poppies self-seed readily and are therefore not difficult to maintain in the rock garden. They are worth a place for the long succession they provide of bright elegant flowers.

P. alpinum, 4in (10cm), forms mounds of prettily divided gray-green leaves. The flowers, which are borne in summer, are white, pink, yellow and orange. There are numerous similar species differing only in minor botanical features. These include: *P. a. kerneri*, yellow; *P. a. rhaeticum*, same colors as *P. a. alpinum*; *P. a. sendtneri*, white; and *P. a. suaveolens*, yellow to red.

P. muyabeanum, 4in (10cm), is in general appearance and color range very like the European *P. alpinum*, but it is said to be longer lived.
Cultivation: These plants are easily satisfied if given sunny well-drained positions. Sow seed in the flowering position.

Penstemon

Although sometimes short-lived, the dwarf species of this large genus of North American plants are worth a place in the rock garden for their profuse summer display of snapdragon-like flowers. Many of those in cultivation have strong similarities

Top *One of the most attractive of all the narcissus species is N. cyclamineus, with its sweptback petals.*

Above N. triandrus albus *is often described as the 'angel's tears' daffodil.*

Above *The low growing* Phlox subulata, *with flowers in shades of lilac, purple or red, makes a showy addition to the rock garden, when it forms hummocks with a tight mat of brilliant flowers in summer.*

and this has led to confusions in their naming. For this reason it is best to read the description in the catalogue, or ask the dealer before buying.

P. davidsonii (syn. *P. menziesii*), 6in (15cm), is a sub-shrubby mat-forming plant with blue-purple flowers that are borne in mid-summer. *P. d. menziesii* (syn. *P. menziesii*) is rather more erect with small toothed leaves and purplish flowers.

P. fruticosus, 12in (30cm), is a shrubby erect perennial with purplish-blue flowers. *P. f. scouleri* (syn. *P. scouleri*) has finely toothed leaves. *P. f. s.* 'Alba' is another lovely white form.

P. heterophyllus, 12in (30cm), is a sub-shrubby species with gray-green leaves and flowers that are bright blue to purple. 'True Blue' is a good pure blue color.

P. laetus roezlii (syn. *P. roezlii*), 10in (25cm), forms a loose mound of downy leaves with rich red flowers.

P. rupicola (syn. *P. newberryi rupicola*), 4in (10cm), has gray-green leaves and carmine flowers.

P. × 'Six Hills', 10in (25cm), is a vigorous hybrid with gray-green leaves and very pretty lilac flowers.

Cultivation: Penstemons require full sun and gritty well-drained soil. Propagate from seed or from cuttings of non-flowering side shoots in summer.

Phlox

The North American dwarf shrubby phloxes are prolific-flowering, mat-forming plants that do well in the rock garden or even planted in a dry wall.

P. adsurgens, 8in (20cm), is a more-or-less erect plant with a creeping root-stock. In spring the plant bears white, pink or purple flowers.

P. douglasii (syn. *P. austromontana*), 4in (10cm), a prostrate species that flowers profusely in late spring and early summer, has numerous good named forms, some of which may be hybrids with *P. subulata.* Desirable forms include: 'Boothman's Variety', mauve; 'Eva', pink; and 'Mabel', mauve-pink.

P. amoena (syn. *P.* × *procumbens*), 8in (20cm), a plant of tufty growth, bears bright purple flowers in early summer.

P. subulata, 4in (10cm), the moss or mountain phlox, flowers profusely in late spring just as the aubrietas are fading. The

flowers are pink or purple but there is great variety of color in the selected forms. These include: 'Alexander's Surprise', salmon pink; 'G. F. Wilson', lavender-blue; 'Temiscaming', crimson; and 'White Delight', pure white.
Cultivation: Plant *P. subulata* and *P. douglasii* in any well-drained soil in a sunny position. *P. adsurgens* needs light shade and a peaty soil, and *P. amoena* a moist soil. Propagate from selected basal cuttings taken in mid-summer.

Picea *see* Conifers.

Pinus *see* Conifers.

Potentilla
The dwarf shrubby cinquefoils are valuable rock garden plants that are easy to grow and have a long flowering season in summer.
P. alba, 4in (10cm), makes a spreading mat of dark green leaves that are silvery on the underside. The flowers, borne from late spring to autumn, are white.
P. aurea, 6in (15cm), makes a loose mat of slightly silvery toothed leaves and bears deep yellow flowers with a darker eye.

There is also a double form *P. a.* 'Plena'. *P. a. chrysocraspeda* (syn. *P. ternata*) has leaves that are less sharply toothed.
P. crantzii (P. alpestris), 8in (20cm), is an attractive yellow-flowering species of which the petals generally have a deeper orange blotch at the base.
P. nitida, 3in (7.5cm), can be shy to flower. It forms silvery mats of foliage and bears stemless flowers of an apple-blossom pink color.
P. tabernaemontani (syn. *P. verna*), 3in (7.5cm), may have a spread of up to 24in (60cm). Although the main season for the bright yellow flowers is late spring, there are odd flowers throughout the summer.
Cultivation: Plant in light, free-draining soil and in full sun. Raise plants from seed or propagate from cuttings.

Primula
Despite being a very numerous group with a wide range of growth patterns, the primulas show strong family traits. The dwarf species are some of the most beautiful. They include several rather difficult alpine plants that are a test of the specialist's skills. However, there are also

Above *The species* Primula allionii *is very small and has rose pink to deep red flowers in spring. There is also a white form.*

Left and opposite *The potentillas, or cinquefoils, are a large genus of plants, some shrubby, but most of them herbaceous in habit.*

Right *Within the vast primula genus there are plants for almost all conditions and many of the compact-growing kinds are happy in cool or shady corners.*

Below Ramonda myconii *produces a rosette of crinkled leaves and purplish flowers in early summer.*

undemanding species and cultivated forms that are excellent plants in the rock garden.

P. allionii, 2in (5cm), makes tight clumps of leaves that are downy and sticky. The flowers, up to 1in (2.5cm) across and ranging in color from white to purple, are borne early to mid-spring.

P. amoena, 6in (15cm), is sometimes listed as *P. altaica,* although this name covers several pink-flowered primulas that are probably of garden origin. All are easy and attractive plants. The true species bears yellow-eyed violet to lavender flowers in mid to late spring.

P. auricula, 6in (15cm), the parent of the show auriculas, has gray-green leaves generally covered with farina. The deep yellow fragrant flowers are borne in spring.

P. edgeworthii, 4in (10cm), has gray-green leaves with wavy margins and bears pale mauve flowers with a yellow eye in late winter and spring. There is a fine white form.

P. farinosa, 6in (15cm), produces heads of pink flowers with yellow centers in early spring. The leaves are powdery white on the underside.

P. frondosa, 6in (15cm), is like a more solid version of *P. farinosa* with heavier powdering of the leaves.

P. marginata, 4in (10cm), a species suitable for a rock crevice, has powdered leaves and in mid-spring bears lavender-blue flowers with a white eye. 'Linda Pope' is a good named form.

P. × *pruhoniciana* (syn. *P.* × *juliana*), 4in (10cm), is the name under which are listed various cultivated hybrids between *P. juliae* and other species. These include: 'Garryarde Guinevere', with bronzed foliage and pink flowers, and 'Wanda', with claret red flowers.

P. × *pubescens,* 4in (10cm), covers the hybrids derived from crosses between *P. auricula* and other primulas. They are generally spring-flowering and have powdery leaves. Good examples include: 'Argus', purple with white centers; 'Harlow Car', cream; 'Mrs J. H. Wilson', large violet; and 'Rufus', brick red.

Cultivation: Most of the hardy primulas listed here should be planted in light shade in humus-rich but well-drained soil. Those with powdery leaves are susceptible to winter damp and when grown outside may need to be given the protection of a glass pane. Propagate from seed sown when ripe and by division.

Pulsatilla

The pulsatillas, of which the pasque flower *(P. vulgaris)* is the best known, show strong family resemblance to the anemones, with which they were previously classified. Their beautiful silky flowers, which are followed by plumed seed heads, are attractively set off by the softly hairy and fern-like foliage.

P. alpina, 12in (30cm), a native of the mountains of Europe, makes a tuft of slightly downy leaves and in late spring and early summer bears white flowers that are tinged blue-pink in the bud. In cultivation the fine yellow-flowered form 'Sulphurea' is more common than the type.

P. halleri, 12in (30cm), is a very similar to the common pasque flower. The leaves are woolly and the flowers deep violet-blue.

P. vernalis, 6in (15cm), makes a small tuft of deep green hairy leaves and in mid-spring produces white flowers with bluish or pinkish markings on the outside.

P. vulgaris, 12in (30cm), a plant of lovely silkiness in leaf, stem, flower bud and seed head. The color is very variable but in the commonest form is mauve. The forms 'Alba', white and 'Rubra', maroon, are pretty.

Cultivation: Plant pulsatillas in well-drained soil in sun. *P. vernalis* may need protection from winter wet. Propagate from seed sown fresh.

Ramonda

The ramondas, a small group of evergreen rosette-forming perennials, are useful shade tolerant plants suitable for planting in rock crevices.

R. myconii, 6in (15cm), has deep green leaves. The mauve flowers with gold stamens, as many as six to a stem, are borne in mid and late spring. There are good pink and white forms.

R. serbica, 4in (10cm), is very like *R. myconii,* but the flowers are slightly different – they are more cup-shaped.

Cultivation: Plant in autumn or early spring in the crevices of shady rock walls. Water must not be allowed to collect in the rosettes but the soil should be reasonably moisture-retentive. Propagate by division, from leaf cuttings taken in summer, or from the very fine seed.

Left *A red form of* Pulsatilla vulgaris, *in which the color is more pronounced on the inside of the petals.*

Below *In this form of* Pulsatilla vulgaris, *the pasque flower, produces outstanding purplish flowers with orange centers.*

Above and right *Rhododendrons are among the most colorful and numerous of shrubs and the dwarf varieties are suitable for both large and small rock gardens.*

Raoulia

The silvery and blue-green mats and cushions formed by these creeping perennials, mainly natives of New Zealand, make an attractive ground cover in the rock garden.

R. australis, ½in (12mm), forms a tight silvery mat up to 12in (30cm) wide, which in summer is dotted with tiny yellow flowers. *Cultivation:* All of these raoulias need sharply drained soil and full sun. Propagate from rooted pieces taken from the edge of the mats.

Rhododendron

Some of the most valuable evergreen and deciduous trees and shrubs for the garden belong to this very large genus. Many are tall-growing plants of woodlands but there are also several low-growing species, which associate well with other dwarf plants, and numerous medium-sized shrubs, which are ideal as the occasional larger component in the rock garden. The hybrids included in this list of evergreen rhododendrons no more than suggest the enormous range of quality plants that have been developed from crossing the species.

R. calostrotum, 24in (60cm), is a plant of gray-green foliage and bright purplish-red flowers, usually borne in pairs, that appear in late spring and early summer.

R. campylogynum, 24in (60cm), has dark glossy leaves and in late spring it bears clusters of bell-shaped purple flowers.

R. 'Carmen', 24in (60cm), forms a spreading bush up to 3ft (1m) wide and produces waxy dark red bells in late spring.

R. 'Cilpinense', 3ft (1m) and of comparable width, makes a rather large plant but is of exceptional beauty. The soft pink flowers have darker markings and are borne in early spring.

R. 'Elizabeth', 24in (60cm), forms a spreading mound about 4ft (1.2m) wide. The scarlet funnel-shaped flowers are borne in mid and late spring.

R. fastigiatum, 30in (75cm), is a twiggy, gray-green shrub that produces lavender-blue flowers in mid-spring.

R. ferrugineum, 3ft (1m), a free-flowering species with dark green leaves that are rusty on the underside, bears clusters of crimson tubular flowers in early summer.

R. forrestii repens, 10in (25cm), a prostrate shrub with leathery leaves that are purplish on the underside, bears crimson flowers, generally singly or in pairs, in mid- and late spring.

R. impeditum, 30in (75cm), is a plant very similar to *R. fastigiatum*, with purple flowers borne at the end of spring.

R. keleticum, 12in (30cm), a dark-green spreading shrub up to 3ft (1m) across,

bears purple flowers singly or in pairs in late spring and early summer.

R. pemakoense, 24in (60cm), forms a spreading mound about 3ft (1m) across. The leaves are dark and glossy above and scaly blue-green on the underside. The purplish flowers are borne in early spring.

R. radicans, 4in (10cm), a tiny prostrate plant, bears purplish flowers singly at the end of spring.

Cultivation: Rhododendrons need a fairly rich acid soil that is moisture-retentive. They tolerate light shade but do well in open positions provided they are sheltered from cold winds. Early-flowering kinds should be planted so that the sun will not strike frosted blossoms before they have had a chance to thaw. An attractive way of growing rhododendrons with dwarf woodland plants and lime-haters is to plant them in raised peat beds. Propagation is generally from cuttings or by layering.

Saxifraga

This large genus of about 350 species is an important one for the rock gardener as it consists in the main of small perennials that are native of mountainous and rocky environments. The range of plants available has been expanded by the cultivation of many hybrids and selected forms. With this genus

Above *A firm, cushion-forming plant,* Saxifraga x 'Jenkinsae', *growing in tufa. The flowers are the palest pink.*

Among the 370 species of saxifraga most are dwarf, tufted perennial and annual plants, ideal for the rock garden. Shown here are: **Top** S. longifolia, **Above** S. grisebachii *and* **Above right** S. cotyledon.

there is scope for the real specialist who wants the challenge of growing to perfection the difficult high alpine species. However, there are plenty of species and hybrids of great charm and beauty that can be grown in the rock garden with very little trouble. It is not intended that the following selection should provide a sampling of all fifteen sections into which the saxifrages have been divided, some of which are of negligible horticultural interest.

S. × *apiculata*, 4in (10cm), forms a cushion up to 12in (30cm) wide of deep green leaves and bears yellow flowers in early spring. This hybrid of the Kabschia section has an excellent white form, 'Alba'.

S. burserana, 2in (5cm), a mat-forming species with blue-green leaves, produces large white flowers singly on reddish stems in early spring. Named forms include 'Gloria' and 'Major', both larger in size than the type.

S. cochlearis, 8in (20cm), has dense rosettes of silvery encrusted leaves from which in mid-summer emerge stems of

white flowers dotted with red. There is a pretty compact form, *S. c.* 'Minor'.

S. cotyledon (syn. *S. pyramidalis*), 24in (60cm), forms large rosettes from which emerge in summer long sprays of fragrant white flowers. *S. c.* 'Caterhamensis' is a handsome form in which the flowers are heavily dotted with red.

S. grisebachii, 8in (20cm), is generally represented in cultivation by the form 'Wisley'. The beautifully patterned rosettes are about 2in (5cm) across. In spring they produce velvety flowering stems of a rich red-purple.

S. × 'Jenkinsae', 2in (5cm), is a vigorous hybrid that makes a low mound of tight gray-green rosettes up to ft (30cm) wide. The pink flowers are borne profusely in early to mid-spring.

S. longifolia, 18in (45cm), forms solitary or small groups of lime-encrusted rosettes. It may take the plant three or so years to produce its splendid arching spray of flowers, and after the plant has flowered in summer the rosette generally dies.

S. moschata, 3in (7.5cm), is a mossy hummock-forming plant that in mid- and late spring bears yellow flowers on wiry stems. The numerous named forms include: 'Atropurpurea', with red flowers, and 'Cloth of Gold', with golden foliage and white flowers. The following are good mossy hybrids derived from *S. moschata*: 'Four Winds', deep crimson; 'Peter Pan', crimson; and 'Pixie', rose-red.

S. oppositifolia, 1in (2.5cm), makes a loose mat and bears purplish flowers in early spring. 'Ruth Draper' and 'Splendens' are vigorous forms with richer coloring than the type.

S. paniculata (syn. *S. aizoon*), 6in (15cm), is a very variable species with a wide distribution in the northern hemisphere. The lime-encrusted rosettes are beautiful in themselves. The flowers, borne in sprays, are white, pink or yellow. *S. p. baldensis* is a particularly attractive miniature that forms a tight mound and bears white flowers.

S. × 'Tumbling Waters', 24in (60cm), a hybrid, one parent of which is *S. longifolia*, has the advantage over this parent that it more consistently makes offsets before the rosette dies after flowering.

S. × 'Southside Seedling', 15in (38cm), probably has as one parent *S. cotyledon*. It is similar to this parent but the flowers are handsomely blotched dark red.

Cultivation: Many saxifrages tolerate or enjoy lime in the soil, which must be well-drained and gritty. Plant in full sun or semi-shade and, where possible, in a rocky crevice. The really dwarf species and hybrids that are rather lost in the rock garden can be seen at their best grown in pots in the alpine house. Propagate from seed, by division or by separating off individual rosettes.

Scilla

Two dwarf species of this large genus of bulbous plants are commonly grown. They are both early and full-flowering plants and, unlike some bulbs, are easily controlled in the rock garden.

S. siberica, 4in (10cm), the Siberian squill, has glossy strap-like leaves that appear before the flowers. The nodding brilliant blue bells are borne three or four to a stem in early spring. 'Spring Beauty' is a particularly vigorous and early form.

S. tubergeniana, 5in (12.5cm), is similar to *S. siberica*, but the flowers are paler with a dark midrib and open as the shoot emerges.

Cultivation: Plant in ordinary well-drained soil in sun or partial shade as soon as bulbs become available in early autumn. Propagation is generally from seed as offsets are not freely produced.

Sedum

The stonecrops, a large genus of succulent perennials, include several of a scale that makes them useful for sunny positions in the rock garden. The five-petalled starry flowers are borne in heads above the rather crowded fleshy leaves.

S. cauticola, 6in (15cm), a deciduous species, has blue-green leaves, and in autumn features heads of lovely deep pink flowers.

S. ewersii, 6in (15cm), is similar to, but more vigorous than *S. cauticola*.

S. rosea (syn. *S. rhodiola*, *Rhodiola rosea*), 1ft (30cm), roseroot, owes its common name to the fact that the dried roots are sweetly scented. This deciduous species makes a rather lax clump of stems closely covered with gray-green leaves and in summer bears compact heads of greenish-yellow flowers.

S. spathulifolium, 4in (10cm), is a hummock-forming evergreen species, the leaves of which often take on a red tinge, producing yellow flowers in early summer. Two good selected forms are 'Capa Blanca', with leaves that are almost white when young; and 'Purpureum', with waxy purplish leaves.

Cultivation: Grow in ordinary well-drained soil in sun. Propagate from seed or from stem cuttings.

Below Sedum cauticola *is a hardy plant that will grow well in the rock crevices or along the top of walls.*

Above and right *The sempervivums or houseleeks, have close rosettes of leaves, some pointed and many with fine, cobweb-like hairs from leaf tip to leaf tip. There are 25 species but many varieties and hybrids can be difficult to identify accurately.*

Sempervivum

The houseleeks are perennial succulents that form dense rosettes of fleshy leaves that are often beautifully tinted and marked. Each rosette may take several years to flower, when it elongates to produce a head of starry flowers. After flowering the rosette dies but the plant is maintained by the annual production of several offsets.

S. *arachnoideum*, 1in (2.5cm), the cobweb houseleek, has tight rosettes, with the leaf tips connected by a web of fine white hairs. The pink flowers are borne in the summer months.

S. × 'Commander Hay', 2in (5cm), is an outstanding hybrid forming large rosettes that are beautifully stained maroon. There are pink flowers in summer.

S. *grandiflorum*, 2in (5cm), has rosettes that are downy and sticky, up to 4in (10cm) across. The flowers, borne in summer on stems up to 6in (30cm) tall, are greenish-yellow in color.

S. *montanum*, 1in (2.5cm), is a very variable alpine species with mid-green hairy leaves and purple flowers. It is the parent of many hybrids.

S. *octopodes*, 1in (2.5cm), is unusual in producing offsets on thread-like stolons

growing from the hair rosettes. The flowers are yellow with red at the base.
Cultivation: Grow in full sun and well-drained soil. A clump of rosettes looks attractive wedged in a rocky crevice. These plants are good subjects for pot cultivation in the alpine house and this is probably the best way to grow *S. arachnoideum* and *S. octopodes*, which resent water on the foliage. Propagate from offsets.

Soldanella

The members of this small genus of true alpines are very much alike, all having nodding bell-shaped flowers with fringed petals hanging over the rounded leathery leaves.

S. alpina, 6in (15cm), has kidney-shaped leaves and in early spring bears lavender-blue flowers.

S. montana, 8in (20cm), has bright green leaves, sometimes purplish beneath, but in most other respects is like a sturdier version of *S. alpina.*

S. villosa, 4in (10cm), a pretty miniature, has hairy leaves and flowers, which are a deep purplish-violet.
Cultivation: Plant in well-drained soil containing plenty of humus in a lightly shaded position. To counteract winter damp cover the ground around plants with sharp grit. This will also help to discourage slugs. Propagate from cuttings or by division.

Thuja *see* Conifers.

Tsuga *see* Conifers.

Above Soldanella montana *is somewhat larger than* S. alpina *and produces attractive, violet-blue flowers in the spring.*

Left Tsuga canadensis *is a fine conifer that thrives well on limestone.*

Tulipa

In addition to the many tall-growing tulips that are used with such brilliant effects in bedding schemes, there are a number of dwarf species and hybrids that are fully at home in the rock garden. Although many of them are richly colored, they have a natural grace that to some extent has been sacrificed in the other more highly cultivated forms.

T. clusiana, 12in (30cm), the candystick tulip, is a very elegant species with gray leaves and white flowers flushed pink on the outside. The flowers open in mid-spring.

T. fosteriana, 12in (30cm), a mid-spring species, has brilliant scarlet flowers which have a basal black blotch that is edged with yellow. There are numerous cultivated forms and hybrids with other dwarf tulips, including *T. greigii*. Two that are particularly desirable are 'Cantata' and 'Princeps'.

T. greigii, 10in (25cm), is conspicuous for the handsome purplish streaking of its leaves as well as for the brilliant scarlet of its flowers, which open in mid-spring. Selected forms or hybrids derived from it include: 'Cape Cod', apricot; 'Oriental Beauty' and 'Red Riding Hood', which are also scarlet in color.

T. kaufmanniana, 8in (20cm), the waterlily tulip, is a compact and early-flowering species with creamy flowers that are flushed pink on the outside. Among those derived from it are the following: 'Heart's Delight', red and pink; 'Shakespeare', warm pink shadings; and 'The First', which is creamy white with carmine and yellow in color.

T. tarda, 6in (15cm), is a striking plant with narrow leaves and flowers opening in mid-spring, with pointed segments that are yellow at the center and white at the points.
Cultivation: Plant in ordinary well-drained soil in full sun. Bulbs are not likely to be long-lived if left from year to year without lifting. Lift in summer after leaves have died down and store in a dry place before replanting in autumn in wet climates. Propagate from offsets. From seed it may take more than five years for bulbs to reach flowering size.

The brilliant colors of the dwarf tulips enhance their delicately shaped blooms. Featured are: **Below** Tulipa fosteriana, *'Dance',* **Bottom** Tulipa greigii, *'Plaisir',* **Bottom right** Tulipa greigii, *'Corsage'.*

Veronica

The speedwells include a number of dwarf perennials that are easy and desirable plants in the rock garden. The shrubby veronicas are now classified under *Hebe* and *Parahebe*.

V. austriaca teucrium (syn. *V. teucrium*), 8–12in (20–30cm), is a very variable sub-species of a clump-forming perennial with a long season of bright blue flowers from mid-summer. There are numerous named forms.

V. cinerea, 4in (10cm), an evergreen forming mats of downy grayish leaves and bearing violet-blue flowers over a long period in summer.

V. gentianoides 'Nana', 6in (15cm), is a useful dwarf form of the rhizomatous border plant. It has dark green leaves and pale blue flowers in early summer.

V. prostrata, 6in (15cm), is a commonly grown prostrate plant with toothed mid-green leaves and deep-blue flowers borne over a long period in summer.

Cultivation: Plant in well-drained but reasonably rich soil in sun. Propagate by division in spring or from cuttings taken in the second half of summer.

Viola

Pansies and violas, the highly developed border plants that have been raised from species of this genus, are generally not treated as perennials and in any event are too gaudy to associate well with other rock garden plants. Some of the species are, however, charming plants well worth a place.

V. aetolica (syn. *V. saxatalis aetolica*), 4in (10cm), is a tufty plant with a long and profuse display of yellow flowers in summer.

V. biflora, 3in (7.5cm), a plant with kidney-shaped mid-green leaves. Its bright

yellow, darkly veined flowers, are borne in glorious profusion throughout the summer months.

V. cornuta 'Minor', 3in (7.5cm), is a prostrate dwarf form of a good border plant. The flowers, borne in summer, are clear blue.

V. labradorica, 4in (10cm), is generally cultivated in the form 'Purpurea', which has purplish foliage and mauve flowers borne in early summer.

Cultivation: The violas are easily satisfied in well-drained soil and positions in full sun or partial shade. Propagate from seed or from selected cuttings of non-flowering basal shoots which should be taken in the mid-summer.

Above left *The veronicas or speedwells, are generally hardy and will grow well in most soils.*

Below left and below *Violas do best in moist, well-drained soil and light shade, and although many pansies now avaiable are best as border plants, there are many attractive dwarf forms for the rock garden.*

INDEX

Picture Credits

Front cover: Michael Warren

Back cover: Harry Smith Horticultural Photographic Collection

Alpine Garden Society: 48(r), 49; Amateur Gardening: 48(l); D. Arminson: 19(br), 25(r), 28(l), 29, 37(cr,br), 46(t), 55(b), 61(r), 68(br), 71(bl); P. Ayers: 26, 37(tl), 62(r), 63(t,b); Paul Beattie: 10/1, 12; K. Beckett: 53(t), 54(b), 59(b); G. D. Bolton: 5; R. J. Corbin: 9(tr,c), 18(r), 27(l), 31(r), 36(t,cl,cr), 37(tr,bl), 39(tl); J. Cowley: 33(br); J. Downward: 20, 53(b); Valerie Finnis: 8(b), 16, 18(l), 24(l), 27(br), 31(l), 34(l), 36(b), 42(t), 43(t), 50(t,b), 52(t), 54(tl), 58(t), 61(l), 62(l), 66(tl); Brian Furner: 32(bl); R. Heath: 17(r); P. Hunt: 43(b), 44(r), 45(t), A. J. Huxley: 66(bl); George Hyde: 39(b); C. Jermy: 30; Leslie Johns: 27(tr), 39(tr), 54(tr); R. Kaye: 24(r), 25(l), 44, 45(b), 56(b), 60(r), 68(tl,tr,bl); Elsa Megson: 34(r); R. Procter: 8(t,c), 35(br), 56(t), 64; Shell: 35(bl); J. Simpson: 69(b); Slide Centre: 42(b); D. Smith: 17(l); Harry Smith Horticultural Photographic Collection: 19(t,bl), 21, 34(l), 35(tl), 46(b), 51(l), 52(b), 55(t), 57(t,b), 58(b), 59(t), 60(l), 65, 66(tr), 67, 69(t), 70(bl,r), 71(t,br); Tourist Photo Library: 70(tl); Michael Warren: endpapers, 13, 28(r).